LOTS OF LOVE . . .

"And now these three remain:
faith hope and love;
but the greatest of these is love."
—I CORINTHIANS 13:13

Gary Wilburn offers up in *Lots of Love*

an antidote to anyone whose life is ruled more by fear than faith and who has yet to extricate themselves from the cat's cradle snares of life's material traps.

In 1997, journalist Mitch Albom wrote *Tuesdays with Morrie*, a heart-warming chronicle of the final months he spent with Morrie Schwartz, his college professor and mentor who was dying of ALS (or Lou Gehrig's disease). As a reporter his world view had been hardened by a career exposed to life's harsh inequities, but Albom was moved by the valuable life lessons tutored by a 78-year-old sociology professor who had dedicated a lifetime of service to shaping young minds.

In the process of imparting his final *vita dictata* to Mitch, Morrie touched the world. Morrie's favorite saying from WH Auden was emphatic: we must "love each other or perish." In the book, Albom is slowly resuscitated to see the world for its possibilities instead of its limitations, and in his personal resurrection, we find hope.

We are fortunate if we find a Morrie Schwartz—a selfless mentor whose life exemplifies the simple truths that "love conquers all" and that "fear and faith cannot possibly coexist in the same space." New Canaan possessed for a brief and magical time our own Morrie Schwartz in the physical and spiritual being of Pastor Gary Wilburn.

Diagnosed with ALS, Gary stepped down in December, 2007, from a dozen-year tenure as pastor of New Canaan's Presbyterian church. His body was beginning to succumb to the debilitating symptoms of his disease, but he and his wife Bev resolved to focus on the gift of life. They moved to a small seaside town in Baja Mexico about 50 miles south of the border to be closer to family, to praise every day and to race time to craft handbooks of living. *The God I Don't Believe In: Charting a New Course for Christianity* and *Lots of Hope* pushed us to reclaim the essential message of Jesus and to embrace the power of hope to change a broken world. Gary's final book in the trilogy—*Lots of Love*—is an urgent and loving testimonial to the simple but fundamental building block of our human and spiritual DNA, that "love is the beginning and the end of our journey."

In a time of great fear and uncertainty, we need these clerics, shamans, priests, and holy persons in our lives to help interpret the deeper meaning of our existence. Gary redirects every ounce of his physical being as an author—a celestial cartographer and guide—tracking our human journey as spiritual beings and interpreting along the way the simple divinity that swirls around us.

Lots of Love achieves spiritual interpretation the way Stephen Hawking fashioned a less complicated lens to the universe in his brilliant book, *A Brief History of the Universe*. How ironic that these extraordinary insights should come from two men whose bodies conspire each day to rob them of their ability to teach us.

Pastor Wilburn understands that society is, by nature, cynical with self-interest but also believes unquestionably in the divine flickering in us like a candle hidden under a bushel basket. Our life's mission is to discover our potential as change agents in this world through the act of loving. Gary guides us as a naturalist might walk us along a gentle mountain path, pointing out the beauty and genius of simple acts of kindness and inviting us to inhale the rich pine-scented humanity that comes from our compassion, humor and values that bind us all as families and communities.

Gary chronicles and celebrates the undeniable goodness of people as he relates vignette after vignette of countless acts of love, gratitude and faith—whether it is in the simple act of passengers giving up their seats on an overbooked flight to make room for soldiers trying to get home on leave from Iraq, to the half-century romantic story of Nate and Theo, a New Canaan couple whose lives and deaths proved as remarkable a testament to inexorable love as any parable.

Each day physical life may ebb out of Gary's body, but his spirit flows through his pen and his glorious fight to bring us all a message of hope at the holiday season. *Lots of Love* is an ornament to be hung on every tree, a candle to be lit on the last night of Hanukkah, an Eid prayer at Ramadan and a strand of lights at the new moon of Diwali.

Gary's message is captured in the haunted words of the great social reformer Charles Dickens and the miraculous self-revelation of George Bailey in "It's A Wonderful Life." *Lots of Love* points out the angels that flit around us each day--our eyes not completely adjusted to see these selfless spirits in the bright light of their kindness.

I can see Gary Wilburn every night in my mind's eye. He is resting in his power chair, silhouetted against a tangerine and blood red sunset praising every minute of a warm, Baja afternoon. Bev is nearby, a soft constant breeze and beloved companion. He smiles and rests—a spiritual being on a human journey. He considers the gifts and challenges that he has been presented in a life advising and leading both affluent and underserved communities. He is at peace.

I call Gary my Captain and have missed him every day that he has been away. He taught his congregation to listen, to seek to understand, to probe for the truth and yes, occasionally to cry with outrage when a seriously flawed society fails to make unconditional love its ultimate priority. He urges us with labored breath that it is through this door of love that we can discover joy and spiritual connection with a power greater than ourselves and rise to heights we humans never thought possible— buoyed by the sheer weightlessness of seeking truth and justice.

Lots of Love illustrates the truth that he would often share with his loving but recidivist and reluctant congregation, "These three things remain: Faith, Hope and Love; but the greatest of these is Love." (I Corinthians 13)

—Michael Turpin, Columnist,
The New Canaan News Review, Connecticut

Dedicated to all my fellow ALS fighters . . .
and those who help them with their daily battle.

LOTS OF LOVE...

GARY ALAN WILBURN

ProgressivePub
Stamford, CT

ISBN: 978-0-9701374-3-2

ProgressivePub
Stamford, CT
For information, email contactus@ProgressivePub.com

Cover art by Sean Wilburn and Kent La Gree
sean@wilburnconsulting.com

Back cover photo of Gary and Bev Wilburn by Erin Dunigan

Book design by Cheryl Mirkin,
CMF Graphic Design

Printed in the United States of America

CONTENTS

LOTS OF LOVE . . . FOR CHRISTMAS

ACKNOWLEDGMENTS

I wish to thank my publisher and friend
Meyrick Payne of ProgressivePub,
my copyeditor Gail Linstrom without whose help
I could not have done this, and my graphic designer
Cheryl Mirkin of CMF Graphic Design.

PROLOGUE

"These three remain: Faith, Hope and Love;
but the greatest of these is Love."
—I CORINTHIANS 13

This book completes my trilogy. In *The God I Don't Believe In: Charting a New Course for Christianity*, I wrote of the urgency of reclaiming the essential message of Jesus. In *Lots of Hope*, I wrote of the power of Hope to change the world. In this third volume, *Lots of Love*, I offer examples of concrete ways in which Love is to be the beginning and the end of our journey.

I am grateful to so many of you around the country who have written me expressing your thanks and telling me of ways in which your lives have been enriched through these pages. What insights do any of us have that we did not first receive through others?

It is my hope that in the days ahead our great nation will show an even greater resolve to "double the heart's might" to make the world a safer, saner, and more compassionate place for all of its inhabitants.

LOTS OF LOVE . . .
Gary

Gary can be reached at Gary@ProgressivePub.com

LOTS OF LOVE . . . FOR EVERY DAY

CHAPTER 1

YOU DON'T SING ME LOVE SONGS ANYMORE . . .

"Love is patient and kind;
Love is not jealous or boastful;
It is not arrogant or rude.
Love does not insist on its own way;
It is not irritable or resentful;
It does not rejoice in wrong,
But rejoices in right.
Love bears all things,
Believes all things,
Hopes all things,
Endures all things.
Love never ends . . .
So Faith, Hope and Love abide, these three,
But the greatest of these is Love."
—I Corinthians 13:4-8a, 13

With all the hoopla in the media these days about sex, love, and marriage in private, public, and cyberspace, I thought it might be fun to begin with a "Top 10 List." This is not from David Letterman but rather the Latter Day Saints.

Here, then, are the "Top 10 Biblical Ways to Acquire a Wife":

#10 Find an attractive prisoner of war, bring her home, shave her head, trim her nails, and give her new clothes. Then she's yours. (Deuteronomy 21:11-13)

#9   Find a prostitute and marry her. (Hosea 1:1-3)

#8   Go to a party and hide. When the women come out to dance, grab one and carry her off to be your wife. (Judges 21:19-25)

#7   Cut 200 foreskins off your future father-in-law's enemies, and get his daughter for a wife. (I Samuel 18:27)

#6   Become the emperor of a huge nation and hold a beauty contest. (Esther 2:3-4)

#5   When you see someone you like, go home and tell your parents, "I have seen a . . . woman; now get her for me." (Judges 14:1-3)

#4   Kill any husband, and take his wife (prepare to lose four sons, though). (II Samuel 11)

#3   Wait for your brother to die. Take his widow. (It's not just a good idea; it's the law). (Deut. 25:5-10)

#2   Don't be so picky. Make up for quality with quantity. (I Kings 11:1-3)

Finally, the most popular "Biblical Way To Acquire A Wife" is:

#1   "A wife? Are you kidding me?" (I Corinthians 7:32-35)[1]

Well, there you have it. A definite gender bias, but that's the way it was in Bible times.

When you cut through our popular obsession with sex and scandal to a genuine concern about ethics, you have to conclude that something is terribly askew with our values today. Despite all of our talk about "family values," many marriages and life-partnerships are not fairing too well. The words may still be there, but the music has long since faded away.

As Barbra Streisand and Neil Diamond sang:

You don't bring me flowers
You don't sing me love songs.
You hardly talk to me anymore
When I come through the door at the end of the day. . . .

It used to be so natural to talk about forever.
But 'used to be's' don't count anymore
They just lay on the floor 'til we sweep them away. . . .

So you think I could learn how to tell you good-bye.
You don't say you need me.
You don't sing me love songs.
You don't bring me flowers anymore.[2]

Perhaps the Beatles were wrong. Perhaps love is not all we need. Perhaps what we need is to live into the words of a different love song.

I cannot tell you how many hundreds of times I have heard the 13th Chapter of I Corinthians read at weddings. The reason is, I think, that it speaks to something deep in the human spirit. Without love, we are nothing. With love, we have everything. Love is even greater than faith or hope. The greatest of all is love.

This beautiful, rhythmic poetry stands alongside the great literature of the world. It has been called "A Hymn to Love." It is written in calligraphy and hung in public places. It is lovely. But it is not often understood nor acted upon. When St. Paul wrote these words, they were not to be read at a wedding; they were to be read to a meeting of a conflicted congregation, caught up in a distorted spirituality, engaged in intense power struggles.

To be sure, they are beautiful words, but they are not written to idealize the concept of love or to praise its virtues. They are addressed to a quarrelsome people who cannot get along with each other, "who need to know that their fervent religiosity isn't worth a tinker's [darn] apart from a new relationship to one another, apart from love."[3]

In other words, people like many of us: folks who need to reassess their relationships with one another, whether in a life partnership, a local church, or any other social contract. For those first readers, the issue was self-centered pride and boasting by some who claimed to be more "spiritual" than the others, or more "important" because of their particular giftedness. Their experience was not unlike any board or committee on which you and I have served—nor unlike many marriages or partnerships of today.

There comes a time when flowers and love songs just don't do it anymore. When that happens and "used to be's just lay on the floor," what does true love entail? Paul tells us in I Corinthians.

First, *love is essential.* The first three verses make it clear that spiritual language, theological insight, courageous faith, extravagant generosity, and even martyr-like suffering does not change a person—without love. It matters not how many flowers we give, how many homes we vacation in, how many degrees we have, how many nonprofit organizations we chair, how many investments we bequeath. If we have not love, we gain nothing for ourselves and less than the best for others. Marriages and partnerships based solely on legalistic performance usually produce guilt, anger, and pretense.

Second, not only is love essential, but *love is practical.* Verses 4-7 make it clear that love is not infatuation, that love is not always lovely, and that romance alone is too shallow to hold during times of stress and conflict. Love is not an abstract idea; it is an action. It refuses to stoop to retaliation, demonstrates patience, shuns competitiveness, resists keeping score, does not demand its own way, and hangs in there for the long haul. Marriage and partnership are the art of two incompatible people learning to live compatibly.

Third, love is essential and practical, and *love is permanent*. The final seven verses of I Corinthians 13 have to do with a shared commitment to live into the future. George Kaufman is said to have told Irving Berlin that the lyrics of his famous song, "Always," ought to be changed from, "I'll be loving you, always," to more realistically, "I'll be loving you, Thursday." Marriage is not only "for as long as we both shall love." It is the commitment which provides the structure necessary for the emotional part of love to grow and come to fruition.

How can someone love that much? They cannot—not without God's help. The secret is found in verse 12: "I will know fully, even as I have been fully known." God is the Unseen Seer, the Unloved Lover, the Unknown One whose own knowledge of us, the partners, or of us, the community of faith, makes our true love possible. It is through doing the best that we can do in the situation, time after time, that God reveals to us resources we never thought we had, to do what we never thought we could, for longer than we ever thought possible.

> *"Love is the filling from one's own,*
> *Another's cup,*
> *Love is the daily laying down*
> *And taking up;*
> *A choosing of the stony path*
> *Through each new day,*
> *That other feet may tread with ease*
> *A smoother way.*
> *Love is not blind, but looks abroad*
> *Through other's eyes;*
> *And asks not, "Must I give?"*
> *But "May I sacrifice?"*
> *Love hides its grief, that other hearts*

And lips may sing;
And burdened walks, that other lives
May buoyant wing.

Hast thou a love like this?
Within thy soul?
'Twill crown thy life with bliss
When thou dost reach the goal."
—AUTHOR UNKNOWN

"Relationships are about adventure with another person—where life unfolds different mysteries with every turn. It needs to be seen as that. Now, some of those adventures are like white water rapids and others are like sailing across a calm lake. But it is still the same adventure. And that adventure begins with God."[4]

I really like the story about the couple celebrating their fortieth wedding anniversary with a quiet dinner for two. The wife lifts her champagne glass and says, "In spite of everything!"

In 2010 my wife, Bev, and I celebrate our fortieth anniversary. Not long by comparison with some marriages, but quite a while in the same covenant with one another. But it is not by luck or accident that we are still together. It is by the grace of God—and hard work. We determined before we got married that divorce was not an option. So, when the feelings ebb and flow, we deal with it and keep going.

I am aware that some couples have given their painful marriages all the energy and love they could muster, yet finally concluded that divorce was the least detrimental option open to them. And they could well be right. I pass no judgment, first because it is not my role to judge, and second because each situation is different. Perhaps some of you are struggling right now to regain what was lost. You need to keep trying, keep working on it, keep on giving it all you've got. Too many partners walk away too soon. But when the papers have been signed, that chapter of your life is closed, and you need to open a new one with all of the faith, hope, love, and courage you can muster.

There is not a day that goes by, but that I thank God for a wife and son whom I love, and who love me "nevertheless"—"in spite of everything!" Saint Valentine might not approve. But Saint Paul would understand. Love at first sight—that's easy to understand. It is after forty years that it becomes a miracle!

CHAPTER 2

LOVE NEVER DIES

Richard was a widower; his wife had suffered a long and painful death from cancer. Then he met Carolyn. They came to love each other and each other's children dearly.

Less than a year into their courtship, Carolyn discovered a lump in her breast. She had gone to the doctor alone and was alone when she received the devastating news: the lump was malignant.

Almost her first thought was of Richard and his children. They had been profoundly wounded by cancer only a few years before. They were still healing from it. How could she bring this terrible thing into their lives again? She called Richard immediately and, without telling him why, simply broke off their relationship. For several weeks she refused his phone calls and returned his letters. But Richard would not give up and begged her to see him.

Finally, Carolyn relented and arranged to meet him to say good-bye. When they met, she could see the deep strain and hurt on his face. Richard gently asked Carolyn why she had broken up with him. Finally, on the verge of tears, she told Richard the truth: that she had found a lump in her breast, that it was malignant, that she had undergone surgery a few weeks before and would begin chemotherapy the following week.

"You and the children have lived through this once already," she told him. "I won't put you through it again."

He looked at her, his jaw dropping. "You have cancer?" he asked. Dumbly, she nodded, the tears beginning to run down her cheeks.

"Oh, Carolyn," he said—and began to laugh with relief. "We can do cancer . . . we know how to do cancer. I thought that you didn't love me!"

Oh, but she did. And they got through it together, happily married.[5]

I remember vividly the day I received a fateful phone call to return home immediately. "Bev needs you right now," said my friend John. Dropping everything I sped home. When I opened the front door I saw Bev surrounded by our close friends, Elizabeth and John, Virginia and Ken.

I held her and said, "What's wrong?" She told me that the doctor had just discovered a lump on the side of her neck. "It may or may not be malignant," she said, "but I have to have it operated on right away." We held each other tightly and cried together, all of us.

When Bev collected herself enough to speak, she said, "I am not afraid for myself Gary. I am afraid for you and Sean."

I immediately responded, "I'll be O.K. You are my life. It's going to be all right. I'll be here for you. We are going to make it through this together."

That surgery did, in fact, reveal a malignant tumor which required a second surgery to remove the entire thyroid. It was especially difficult and potentially life-threatening. Thankfully, the surgery was successful, and Bev has been cancer-free for some years now. But there is not a day that goes by but that we each remember our mortality and vow to celebrate the gift of life.

That first dark night, and ever since, Jesus's promise has been lived out in our marriage and family time and time again. "The Spirit of the Lord is upon me to bring good news to the poor . . . release to the captives and recovery of sight to the blind, to let the oppressed go free. . . ."

"We can do cancer . . . we know how to do cancer! I thought you didn't love me!"

Perhaps you also know these realities down deep in your soul. You have loved another for a lifetime and have shared enough life together for an eternity. You have faced unbelievable challenges and have gone through hell and back together time and time again. You have been strong for the other and have been weak enough to allow the other's strength to come alongside and fill in the gaps. Even though the love of your life may no longer be with you, you have known real love . . . and continue to be buoyed up by it day after dark day.

Love endures. Nothing in life is permanent. But Love never fails.

In his book, *Overcoming Life's Disappointments*, Rabbi Harold Kushner tells of meeting with a young couple to prepare their wedding ceremony. Everything was going well until the prospective bridegroom asked:

"Rabbi Kushner, would you be willing to make one small change in the ceremony? Instead of pronouncing us 'husband and wife till death do us part,' could you pronounce us 'husband and wife for as long as our love lasts'? We've talked about this, and we both feel that if we ever get to the point where we no longer love each other, it's not morally right for us to be stuck with each other and be deprived of any chance for happiness."

Not surprisingly, the Rabbi would not agree to the change.

"I told them that I respected their distaste for hypocrisy, for not wanting to live in a loveless marriage," Kushner writes. "I told them that I could understand their fear of making a total commitment to this marriage because it might hurt too much if it didn't work out. But I warned them that if they didn't enter this marriage on the assumption that it was for keeps, if they moved in together but didn't totally unpack—ready to move out when things got tough—there was no chance that they would be happy together. They would not be committed enough to stay together during the inevitable tough times."[6]

One of the promises two people make to each other in their vows of marriage or holy union is the commitment to stick together through the hard times in the faith that the hard times will one day end and the affection they once felt for each other will reemerge. That may sound like the opposite of love. But no . . . that is the essence of love. "Love never dies."

Love—authentic love—is hard work. Love is a commitment—in sickness and in health, in wealth and in poverty, in the good times and in the hard times. And sometimes it does seem as though it should not be that hard, or take that much work.

"But love endures long after the romance hardens into reality; love finds its fulfillment in diapers and mortgages and college tuition and the messes and complexities of everyday life; love dares to hope and sacrifice despite the disappointments and hurts.

"May each of us dare to love as God loves us: regardless of the

cost and sacrifice, without limit or condition, totally and completely, in the eternal hope that such love will transform us and
those we love in the life of God."[7]

Love never fails.

CHAPTER 3

A LOVE STORY
(FOR NATE AND THEO)

"My beloved speaks and says to me:
'Arise, my love, my fair one,
and come away;
O my dove, in the clefts of the rock,
in the covert of the cliff,
let me see your face,
let me hear your voice;
for your voice is sweet,
and your face is lovely.'
My beloved is mine and I am his."
—SONG OF SONGS 2:10, 14, 16A

Most of us who consider ourselves to be romantics to one degree or another remember that sensitive scene in *Fiddler on the Roof* when Tevia says to his wife, Golde, *"Do you love me?"*

To which a startled and no-nonsense Golde replies: *"Do I love him? For twenty-five years I've lived with him, fought with him, starved with him. Twenty-five years my bed is his. If that's not love, what is!"*

Tevye says: *Then you do love me?"*

Golde responds, *"I suppose I do."*

Tevye, *"And I suppose I love you, too."*

Then together they both sing,

"It doesn't change a thing,

But even so,

After twenty-five years,

It's nice to know."[8]

In the life and teaching of Jesus, nothing is more important than love. Love is the be-all and end-all of life. We were created in love, sustained in love, and are fulfilled in love.

"And now faith, hope, and love abide, these three; and the greatest of these is love."[9]

So, what in the world is love? How would you define it? Let's play a word association game. What word comes to mind when I say "love"? A warm feeling? Friendship? Fear? Intimacy? Sex? Family? Hurt? Hope? What?

Former *Los Angeles Times* columnist Jack Smith reported on how people have struggled to define the word "love." Putting words around the idea of love has been so difficult throughout history that some dictionaries omitted it completely! One early attempt at defining love was made in *The Ladies' Dictionary*, published in 1694:

> "'Tis very much like a light, a thing that everybody knows, and yet no one can tell what to make of it. . . . 'Tis not money, flouncing, searing, fortune, jointure, raving, stabbing, hanging, romancing,

ramping, desiring, fighting, dicing . . . 'though all
these have been, are and still will be mistaken and
miscalled for it. . . . 'Tis extremely like a sigh and
could we find a painter who could draw one, you'd
easily mistake it for the other. . . ."

Personally, I prefer Dr. Scott Peck's definition. In his classic
book, *The Road Less Traveled*, he defines love as "the *will* to extend
one's self for the purpose of nurturing one's own or another's spiritual growth."[10]

Jesus tells us that love is both a command and a promise. While
the command to love one another was not at all new to his fellow
Jews of the day, the priority that Jesus puts on it as being the most
important thing in life is new. Further, the extent of our love for
one another is to be new. We are to love as God has loved us in
Jesus, going the extra mile, giving up our own life if need be.

Love is of such ultimate importance, Jesus says, that it carries
with it the promise that our love for one another will prove to all
people that we are his disciples. Not our doctrine, but our love. In
his final high-priestly prayer for us in John 17, Jesus even goes so
far as to claim that the way we love one another will demonstrate
to the world that God is in Christ, reconciling the world to God's
self.

The fact is, love is not first and foremost a feeling, be it warm
fuzzies or sexual passion or even compassion. As beautiful as those
feelings are, they can hardly be the new commandment our Lord
has given us. Nor can we in our right minds believe that any
amount of "feeling good" or "feeling turned on" by somebody else
is enough for the world to know that God was in Christ, reconciling the world to God's self. The church was never intended to be
a hot tub and massage parlor for stroking our emotional pleasure
centers.

Love is an act of the will, not a product of the glands or hor-
mones. We choose to love. We do not have to love. Love does not
just happen. We do not fall into love like we might fall into an ele-

vator shaft. Love involves effort in extending our limits, going beyond ourselves. It always means taking the extra time or walking the extra mile.

And wouldn't you know, love is a strangely circular process. What goes around comes around. As we act lovingly to another, we cannot help but nurture our own spirit. As we act out of our truest self, we cannot help but nurture the spiritual growth of others. The poet Roy Croft put it this way:

> "I love you
> Not only for what you are,
> But for what I am
> When I am with you.
>
> I love you
> Not only for what
> You have made of yourself,
> But for what
> You are making of me.
>
> I love you
> For the part of me
> That you bring out;
> I love you for putting your hand
> Into my heaped-up heart,
> And passing over all the foolish, weak things
> That you can't help
> Dimly seeing there,
> And for drawing-out
> All of the beautiful belongings
> That no one else had looked
> Quite far enough to find.
>
> I love you because you
> Are helping me to make

Of the timber of my life
Not a tavern
But a temple;
Out of the works of my every day
Not a reproach
But a song.

I love you
Because you have done
More than any creed
Could have done to
Make me good,
And more than any fate
Could have done
To make me happy. . . ."

This is precisely the love that dear friends and longtime members of our church in New Canaan, Connecticut, Nate and Theo Becker, shared with each other for over fifty years. It was that mutual, outgoing, other-focused love for life, family, friends, the beauty of the earth, and God which kept them together hand-in-hand over the years. When Theo died, it was a shock to all of us.

Theo's service was truly a celebration and thanksgiving of her life and love. After the service we had a reception for Nate which seemed to just keep getting better the longer it went on. One after another of the guests told Nate stories of how their lives had been changed by having known Theo and him. Nate would listen carefully to each one, share in their joy, and thank them for coming.

The following morning we had planned an interment for Theo at Lakeview Cemetery. All of the boys and their families were there to say their final goodbyes. Their son Ken picked Nate up and drove him to the cemetery. When they arrived at the cemetery and came within sight of Theo's gravesite at the top of the hill, Nate quietly dropped his head to the side and silently passed away in the back seat of the car.

EMTs, ambulance, police, all were there within minutes. The New Canaan response team was there immediately, but to no avail. Nate had died only a stone's throw from the love of his life.

There, in the beauty of that bright sunny day, with the piercing wind whistling through the trees, and the sounds of newborn birds and mallards on the waters of the pond, each of us cried out to God in wrenching bursts of pain and disbelief. *"No!" "Not Nate, too!" "Oh God, not Nate!"*

When all that could be done was done, loving, trembling hands ever so carefully placed Nate alongside his wife's open gravesite, with his arm enfolded around her urn of ashes. As they had been together in life, so they were in death. I commended the two of them into the Everlasting Arms of the God who gave them to us, and committed their bodies to their final resting place "in sure and certain hope of the resurrection to eternal life, through our Lord Jesus Christ."

Herein was love: two beautiful souls joined together through the years of over half-a-century by a love that would not let them go. Always they had walked together—hand-in-hand, arm-in-arm, heart-in-heart—knowing what the other was thinking and feeling without needing to say a word. Now they would enter eternity together bound inseparably by that same love.

In some ways, it could not have been worse. In other ways, it could not have been better. Perhaps they, more than we, knew what they must do. And there, in that sacred place, they held one another's hand, and beautifully, mystically merged with the Universe and with their Creator.

Shakespeare had it right:

> *"Love's not Time's fool, though rosy lips and cheeks*
> *Within his bending sickle's compass come;*
> *Love alters not, with his brief hours and weeks,*
> *But bears it out even to the edge of doom.*
> *If this be error and upon me proved,*
> *I never writ, nor no man ever loved."*[11]

"Who will separate us from the love of Christ? Will hardship, or distress, or persecution, or famine, or nakedness, or peril, or sword? No, in all these things we are more than conquerors through him who loved us. For I am convinced that neither death, nor life, nor angels, nor rulers, nor things present, nor things to come, nor powers, nor height, nor depth, nor anything else in all creation, will be able to separate us from the love of God in Christ Jesus our Lord."[12]

Ours is the loss, not theirs. You and I still have time to love. Whose hand needs yours to hold today? Whose heart needs yours to cheer? Whose ears need to hear your voice? Whose eyes need to read your name, "With love"?

Life is all too short. But love never ends. So, with Robert Browning, I invite you to:

"Grow old along with me!
The best is yet to be,
The last of life,
For which the first was made.
Our times are in His hand
Who saith, 'A whole I planned,
Youth shows but half;
Trust God: see all, nor be afraid!'"[13]

I invite you to make this your daily prayer:

"Oh, God, until we reach Life's ebbing tide,
May we in perfect love and peace abide.
And when Life's sun shall set beyond the hill,
May we go hand-in-hand, together still."[14]

Amen.

CHAPTER 4

THE LABOR PANGS
OF LOVE

They say that having a child is the most traumatic stress to a relationship. Well, let me tell you, marrying off that child runs a close second! Babies only need milk and love. Engaged couples need engagement parties and "Meet the Parents" dinners and guest lists and wedding sites and rehearsal dinners and restaurant receptions and gowns and kilts and flowers and honeymoons and money . . . LOTS OF MONEY!

I figured that our only son Sean's marriage would be a "no brainer," since, after all, I am a professional clergyman, a former seminary professor of marriage counseling, and have performed weddings of just about every size and shape for nearly 1,000 brides and grooms. So, this should be a "cake walk," right? NOT!

The surprises began with a massive electrical storm in the middle of our outdoor "get-acquainted with the families dinner" with the bride, Joanie, her mother, and sisters at our house and continued non-stop until the newlyweds left on their honeymoon.

If it is true that a sailor's two happiest days are the day he buys his boat and the day he sells it, then a parents' happiest days must be the day their children announce their marriage and the day the final bill is paid!

As the English statesman, John Selden, put it, "Of all actions of a man's life, his marriage does least concern other people; yet of all actions of our life, it is most meddled with by other people."

Still and all, as difficult as they are at times, families are the essential building block for a truly human life. Didn't Margaret Mead, the great anthropologist, put it right when she said, "No matter how many communes anybody invents, the family always creeps back."

We are who we love—especially our family and friends. It is important to remember that in following Jesus's model, the church has never taught that marriage is necessary for faithful or fulfilled human life. Indeed, while life in the community of faith is considered essential for wholeness and health, there are varieties of interpersonal relationships and loving and committed partnerships.

But for most people, marriage and family life is the crucible in which our lives are formed, our values are forged, and our life purposes are focused. It takes the presence of another person to "draw out all of the beautiful belongings that no one else had looked quite far enough to find." If we are to climb the ladder from where we are to where God wants us to be, one of the things we must do is outgrow the habit of relying on ourselves alone and learn to let other people into our lives.

"Our survival depends on the healing power of love, intimacy and relationships." We need to feel loved. But we also need to give love, to make a difference in someone's life. Love involves nourishing someone else's soul, not just finding someone willing to nourish ours. As one person put it, "I used to feel I was loved because I was special. Now I feel special because I *am* loved and because I *can* love."[15]

Delores Curran surveyed over five hundred teachers, pastors, pediatricians, counselors, and social workers regarding family strengths. She describes in her book the top fifteen traits of healthy families. Those families communicate and listen. They affirm and support each other. The healthy family teaches respect for others and develops a sense of trust. The healthy family has a sense of play and humor, shares leisure time, and balances interaction among members. There is a sense of shared responsibility and a shared religious core. The healthy family teaches a sense of right and wrong and values service to others. They respect each other's privacy, admit to and seek help with problems, and have a strong sense of family in which rituals and traditions abound.[16]

Paul Tsongas was a young and rising member of the U.S. Senate. Learning he had cancer made him reevaluate the time he had been spending with his wife and children, compared with the time he spent at work. After spending a rare evening at home with them, he realized that with the 24/7 schedule he was keeping, the next night like this would probably be several years in the future. After this sobering realization he made this observation: "Nobody on his deathbed ever said, *'I wish I had spent more time on my job.'*"

One of my favorite columnists is Ellen Goodman of *The Boston Globe*. She and her best friend, novelist Patricia O'Brien, wrote in their book, *I Know Just What You Mean*, "Friendship has no biological purpose, no economic status, no evolutionary meaning." But "a new friend can reintroduce a woman to herself, allowing her to look at herself with a new pair of eyes and a different mindset.... Flaws can be recast as strengths, self-doubts lifted by acceptance. . . . Friends are more likely than family to encourage change."[17]

Jesus taught as much in his Great Commandment to "Love the Lord your God with all your heart, soul, mind and strength, and to love your neighbor as yourself."[18] That mandate is a call to a profound unity in which we are all part of one divine love. "First, when we direct our whole beings toward God, we will find our [friends and] neighbor[s] and ourselves right in the heart of God. Second, when we truly love ourselves as God's beloved children, we will find ourselves in complete unity with our neighbor and with God. And third, when we truly love our neighbor as our brother and sister, we will find, right there, God and ourselves in complete unity. . . . All is one: the heart of God, the hearts of all people, and our own heart."[19]

As Martin Buber, the great Jewish philosopher, said: God is found in relationships. God is not only found *in* people, God is found *between* people. "Both love and true friendship are more than a way of knowing that we matter to someone else. They are a way of mattering to the world, bringing God into a world that would otherwise be a vale of selfishness and loneliness." [20]

We are who we love! So, really, what's a little parental stress and strain and life savings compared to the joy of participating in one of God's grand schemes of rebuilding the world?

So, to Sean and Joanie, we say, "God Bless You. Here's mom and dad's *L' CHAIM TO LIFE!*"

CHAPTER 5

WHERE LOVE REIGNS

One day, a poor boy, who was selling goods from door-to-door to pay his way through school, found he had only one thin dime left, and he was hungry. He decided he would ask for a meal at the next house. However, he lost his nerve when a lovely young woman opened the door. Instead of a meal he asked for a drink of water! She thought he looked hungry so she brought him a large glass of milk. He drank it so slowly, and then asked, *"How much do I owe you?"*

"You don't owe me anything," she replied. *"Mother has taught us never to accept pay for a kindness."*

He said, *"Then I thank you from my heart."*

Howard had been ready to give up and quit. But as he left that house, he not only felt stronger physically, but his faith in God and humanity was strong as well.

Many years later that same young woman became critically ill. The local doctors were baffled. They finally sent her to the big city, where they called in specialists to study her rare disease. Dr. Kelley was called in for the consultation. When he heard the name of the town she came from, a strange light filled his eyes. Immediately he rose and went down the hall of the hospital to her room. Dressed in his doctor's gown he went in to see her. He recognized her at once. He went back to the consultation room determined to do his best to save her life. From that day on he gave special attention to her case. After a long struggle, the battle was won, and she was well.

Dr. Kelly requested the business office to pass the final bill to him for approval. He looked at it, then wrote something on the edge . . . and the bill was sent to her room. She feared to open it, for she was sure it would take the rest of her life to pay for it all. Finally she looked at it, and something caught her attention on the side of the bill. She read these words: *"Paid in full with one glass of milk."* (Signed by) *Dr. Howard Kelly*

"I give you a new commandment, that you love one another. Just as I have loved you, that you also should love one another." John 13:31-35

Jesus's words in the Gospel of John are so simple. To be known as a disciple, a follower of Jesus, all that is required is to love one another. Nothing is said about performing certain rituals, nor believing certain doctrines or dogmas, nor being of a particular religion, nor following certain rules and regulations. "God is love, and those who abide in love abide in God, and God abides in them."[21]

In the life and teaching of Jesus, nothing is more important than love. Love is the be-all and end-all of life. We were created in love, sustained in love, and are fulfilled in love. "And now faith, hope, and love abide, these three; but the greatest of these is love."[22]

Medical doctor and Ph.D. David R. Hawkins puts it this way: "Loving is a state of being. It's a forgiving, nurturing, and supportive way of relating to the world. Love isn't intellectual and doesn't proceed from the mind; love emanates from the heart. It has the capacity to lift others and accomplish great feats because of its purity of motive. Love takes no position," he says, "and thus is global, rising above separation. It's then possible to be 'one with another,' for there are no longer any barriers. Love is therefore inclusive and expands the sense of self progressively. Love focuses on the goodness of life in all its expressions, and augments that which is positive—it dissolves negativity by recontextualizing it, rather than by attacking it."[23]

"Where love reigns," insisted the great psychotherapist, Carl Jung, "there is no will to power; and where the will to power is paramount, love is lacking. The one is but the shadow of the other. . . ." "Love never claims . . . it ever gives."[24]

Perhaps no one can teach us what love is better than children. Children have a hard-wired connection to love. They come by it naturally. Their roots go down deep into it. There is no "will to power over others" with most children because they naturally love one another as equals. And they treat each other as they would want to be treated themselves.

Allow me to make a suggestion to you who are parents of young children. My guess is that many of you tuck your son or daughter into bed at night and ask them, *"How was your day?"* Suppose you were to go about it a little differently. What if you were to ask them, *"Where did you meet God today?"* And then let them tell you: *"A teacher helped me." "My friend let me pet his dog." "I helped a homeless person in the park." "I saw a tree with lots of flowers on it." "I let my friend ride my bike."*

"I was really thirsty and a nice lady gave me a glass of milk."

Then, when your child is finished, tell her or him where *you* met God that day. So that before your children drop off to sleep, the stuff of the day becomes the substance of prayer.[25]

It even works with adults. Because where love reigns in a home, separation doesn't have one thin dime of a chance.

CHAPTER 6

DON'T YOU THINK
IT'S TIME WE
WENT UPSTREAM?

My first point is this: At the core of the Christian faith is the simple but profound assertion that God loves you just as you are! Nothing you or I could ever do will change the heart of God toward us. Regardless of who we are, or where we came from, or what we have or have not done with our lives, God loves us. Period. End of sentence.

It stands to reason, then, that our most natural response to the reality of being loved by God is to love God back. "Thou shalt love the Lord thy God with all thy heart, mind, and soul. This is the first and greatest commandment," said Jesus. **This is the personal side of the gospel.**

The second greatest commandment, Jesus told us, is to love others. Not just those we know and love, but those whom we do not know and therefore may not love. And not merely love them with a polite kind of acceptance, but love them with the same self-giving love with which God has loved us. **This is the social side of the gospel.**

I believe that God's love for the world has two arms. We might say that the right arm of God's love is "personal transformation." The left arm of God's love is "public transformation." These are the two arms with which God hugs the world: personal and public transformation. As Tom Stella puts it, "The bottom line of all the great religions of the world is love. The love of God, neighbor (whether friend or foe), and one's self is the defining characteristic of all people who are serious about their ultimate destiny and their relationship with the Divine."[26]

"Where charity and love are, there is God." But we have reduced the grand concept of charity to the miniscule realm of charitable hand-outs to the poor and needy, good gestures that make us feel good in doing good. But the irony in that kind of charity is that it fosters deeper dependence upon the giver rather than empowering people with the resources to rebuild their own lives.

Christianity is not primarily a religion of *right belief*. It is also, if not more so, a religion of *noble behavior*. That love of God *for* us has to find its way *through* us to others.

Divine charity is not merely a matter of giving to or helping others. It is about laying down our lives for them, setting aside our rights for them, refusing to exercise our power over them, not being content with what we are and have until all people have the same opportunity to attain that same contentment. True love, for a person or an ideal, always involves a commitment.

I love an old story about a chicken and a pig. The two of them were out for a stroll on a hot summer morning. After a long and tiresome time they came upon a restaurant with a sign that read "Ham and Eggs." The chicken said, "Let's go in; I'm starving." The pig responded adamantly, "Not me, pal. For you it's merely a question of involvement, but for me it's a matter of total commitment!" I would hazard a guess that for most of us, love is a matter of involvement, not total commitment.

This is the problem with a one-armed hug! You know those socially-correct hugs we feel obliged to give one another on occasion (often with a little pat on the back)? It's well-meaning, but it just doesn't quite make it. As much as I try, I cannot hug you completely with just one arm. It's like clapping with one hand. It just does not work. I need to put both arms around you for you to know that I really do care about you.

"Charity and kind deeds are always good; there will always be need for help. But the individualization of compassion means that one does not ask how many of the suffering are in fact victims. . . . Justice means asking why there are so many victims and then doing something about it."[27]

That's why Tom Stella reminds us of the oft-told story of the two missionaries who left their compound to walk to a nearby river. "As they stood watching the current, they saw a dead body floating downstream. They waded into the water, retrieved the body, dug a grave, and buried it. They then returned to the river and saw two more bodies. After burying them, they returned again and saw four bodies. It was then that one of them turned to the other and said, 'Don't you think it's time we went upstream?'"[28]

Charity binds wounds and buries bodies. Justice seeks to prevent the cause of the wounds. We can each be effective at the personal level as we do what we can to treat the symptoms of the many problems around us, social and spiritual. But we need to band together as a church, a temple, a mosque, a community, a country, and a common world to remedy the causes of the pain and prejudice, the hatred and horror, the starvation and stockpiling, the ignorance and illiteracy, inequality and injustice, the disease and death plaguing all of us all over the world.

Don't you think it's time we went upstream? Love is not merely personal; it is public. Love is not merely emotion, not merely charity, and not merely justice. It is all of these together, embraced by all people, whatever religion, race, culture, or condition.

Karl Marx understood the difference between charity and justice. One evening he said to a group of assembled Christians, "You Christians have a vested interest in unjust structures which produce victims to whom you then can pour out your hearts in charity."

Some people make the same accusation about America. But I do not agree. I think the heart of America is good and at its best wants the best for all people, not only the privileged, and not only Americans. But I do agree that it is all too easy for us to put temporary bandages on wounds which are the result of institutional neglect and which will never be healed until our public institutions and social systems put as much emphasis on the common good as they do the bottom line.

Don't you think it's time we went upstream? If religion ends with the individual, it ends! St. Paul summarizes his thesis on love in I Corinthians 13: "Now abide faith, hope, and love, these three; but the greatest of these is love."

"Nothing that is worth doing can be achieved in our lifetime;" claimed Reinhold Neibuhr, "therefore we must be saved by hope. Nothing which is true or beautiful or good makes complete sense in any immediate context of history; therefore we must be saved by faith. Nothing we do, however virtuous, can be accomplished alone; therefore we are saved by love. No virtuous act is quite as virtuous from the standpoint of our friend or foe as it is from our standpoint. Therefore we must be saved by the final form of love which is forgiveness."[29]

May God forgive us, enlighten us, and empower us to change not only ourselves, but also the basic structures of our society and the world, for our good and for God's glory.

CHAPTER 7

THE CIRCLE OF LOVE

Writing for *The New York Times*, Clyde Haberman entitled his column, "Integration, One Sunday at a Time." "More than 40 years have passed since the Rev. Dr. Martin Luther King Jr. described 11 a.m. on Sunday as the most segregated hour of the week, and in all that time not much has changed," he said. "Look around on any given Sunday. Worship remains essentially a tribal act. Whites pray here, blacks pray there, and that, you might say, is that."[30]

"There are remarkably few congregations in this country that are truly integrated," said Reverend William Tully, the rector of St. Bartholomew's Episcopal Church in New York City. "It's not just because of housing patterns or income. The same is true outside of church. Go to a New York restaurant of any note, or visit a Broadway theatre, or attend a concert at Lincoln Center or a movie at Lincoln Square. . . . You might as well have Jim Crow laws for all the integration that is taking place," he continued.

Picture a bicycle wheel. The first circle of love and the strongest part of the bicycle wheel is the hub. The hub is not the largest, nor the most visible part, but it is the strongest. All the spokes emanate from that center. Our primary identity is like the hub of a wheel: it is not in our race or our income or our positions or our possessions. It is in who we are: human beings created in the image of God, who share a common life with our Creator and with all of creation.

Then comes the second circle of love, which, like the inner rim of a wheel, connects each of us to all of us. Love creates relationship and the strength of shared goals and purposes. The word Jesus uses for friend is "phileo." It implies the intimacy of blood relationship or shared purpose. Love is first and foremost God's decision for us. But then it is our decision to respond to God by investing our lives in others.

Like Robert Burns' poem has it,

> *"But deep this truth impress'd my mind—*
> *Thro' all His works abroad,*

The heart Benevolent and kind,
The most resembles God."[31]

Our churches must not be refuges for those escaping the world to be with their own kind. They must be "extended families" for those who are unique and don't necessarily fit the molds. In a culture which values homogeneity, we must value differences and aspire to accept one another for who and what we are. We need to encourage the kind of openness and authentic humanness which breaks down barriers of fear and builds bridges of trust and love.

The first disciples of Jesus were convinced that the standard of behavior he expected of his followers was love for their neighbors and the stranger, whether or not there was any prior common bond with them. As followers of Jesus we are bound to treat our fellow human beings with kindness and respect. The way we treat one another is more important than the way we express our beliefs.

"Make love your aim," St. Paul told the Corinthians—not orthodoxy of doctrine, nor purity of behavior, nor perfection of religious practice. If "God is love, and the one who abides in love abides in God," as the Bible says, then revelation is in the relationship, not in the creed. The integrity of love is more important than the purity of dogma.

"Greater love has no one than this," Jesus said, "that a man lay down his life for his friends."

As Martin Luther King, Jr. explained it, "If the church of today does not recapture the sacrificial spirit of the early church, it will lose its authentic ring, forfeit the loyalty of millions, and be dismissed as an irrelevant social club with no meaning for the twentieth century." How much truer this is for the twenty-first century.

As Bill Coffin put it: "God's love is visionary. . . . It doesn't seek value; it creates it. Christians recognize their value as a gift rather than an achievement: it is not because we have value that we are loved, but because we are loved that we have value."[32]

Some years ago I lost a dear friend, mentor, and colleague, Dr.

David H. C. Read, the Senior Minister of the Madison Avenue Presbyterian Church in New York City. Our friendship went back many years and across many miles, from my pastorates in Los Angeles to my installation as Senior Pastor of the First Presbyterian Church of New Canaan, Connecticut, where he preached what had to be the longest Installation Sermon in the history of the Presbyterian Church! Our visits over the years both in his home and mine were always stimulating. We would discuss what we were reading, thinking, and preaching. We would challenge each other's assumptions and explore how we might better connect the Word with the World. David was one of God's special people in my life. His confidence in me helped me to stand taller, and his belief in me helped me to lift my sights to greater heights and to take on greater challenges.

He tells the story of coming to New York in 1956, after being a parish minister in The Church of Scotland, a prisoner of war in a German concentration camp, Moderator of the General Assembly, and Chaplain to the Queen. Some years ago, after years of celebrated preaching, David came to the conclusion that most preachers have "got God wrong," as he put it. Instead of proclaiming a God who laid impossible demands on his children, rewarding the obedient and punishing the rebellious, we should be joining the party that celebrates the God of unconditional love who is calling us home. That love knows no barriers of race or class or ideology. We are loved and accepted by Love itself—whether or not we choose to claim our acceptance.

My final visit with my friend found him confined to bed and suffering memory loss from a stroke that had paralyzed the left side of his body. He drank tea this time, rather than Famous Grouse Scotch Whiskey, and found it too difficult to smoke any of his favorite pipes.

When it was time for me to leave, we embraced as always, kissed one another on the cheek, and I said to him, "The Lord be with you, my friend."

Then in a painful but beautiful act he made the sign of the cross, from his head to his heart. He looked into my soul with his clear, radiant eyes, and with faltering words said, "And also with you, Gary."

Love doesn't seek value, it creates it! Revelation is in the relationship.

Thanks be to God.

CHAPTER 8

PUTTING LOVE
TO WORK

An English newspaper asked this question: "Who are the happiest people on earth?" These were the four prize-winning answers:

- A craftsman or artist whistling over a job well done,
- A little child building sand castles,
- A mother, after a busy day, bathing her baby, and
- A doctor who has finished a difficult and dangerous operation and saved a human life.

No millionaires among these, one notices. No kings or emperors. Riches and rank, no matter how the world strives for them, do not make happy lives.

Money Magazine reported the story of former CBS news correspondent Doug Tunnell. Tunnell decided a few years ago that television news shows were too willing to jettison journalistic principles to rev-up ratings. Rather than wallow in disappointment, he laid the groundwork for a new career. Today Tunnell earns a comfortable living making wine from the grapes he grows at his vineyard in Newberg, Oregon, and feels again the pride and passion he experienced as a journalist. "I feel like the luckiest guy in the world," he said.[33]

There is a growing consensus that one's God-given vocation is most often linked to one's employment. It is derived from one's gifts given in service to meet the needs of one's neighbors, to fulfill the purposes of God, and to bring about social change.[34]

"Work is love made visible," wrote Kahlil Gibran in *The Prophet.*

Most Americans earn, or have earned, their living through some form of business. Yet the work of business is often thought of as being vulgar, philistine, and morally suspect, as though its only purpose is to make the almighty dollar (and more of them than anyone else). One reason for this is television. Prior to 1965, businessmen were portrayed as good guys twice as often as bad guys. (Remember Jimmy Stewart in *It's A Wonderful Life*? There was a humane, compassionate, and, would you believe it, likable banker.) In the 1970s this ratio was reversed—two villains for every good guy. By 1980 a majority of the CEOs portrayed on prime time television committed felonies. Respectable business people were by then committing 40 percent of the murders and 44 percent of vice crimes like drug trafficking and pimping.

Contrary to that distorted perception, I believe that one can find one's Divine calling, one's vocation, in business, as well as most every other choice of work. As Michael Novak put it in his book on *Business as a Calling*, "Half of the pleasure from the business calling derives from a sense that the system of which it is a part is highly beneficial to the human race, morally sound, and one of the great social achievements of all time. The other half is personal—finding purpose and meaning in what one does."[35] There are countless examples:

John Templeton, founder of the Templeton Growth fund and perhaps the greatest investor of our time, told *Forbes Magazine* recently that from the time he was young through his years at Yale and Oxford as a Rhodes scholar, he had wanted to become a missionary. "I realized that they had more talent as missionaries than I did," he says. "But I also realized that I was more talented with money than they were. So I decided to devote myself to helping the missionaries financially. His financial success has been amazing. So also has been his worldwide philanthropy. John Templeton is a great humanitarian. His international prizes for social betterment are well known. John Templeton devotes time every day to prayer. He treats his lifetime occupation, global investing, as a vocational calling from God.

Kenneth Lay, once the highly respected chairman and CEO of the largest natural gas company in the U.S., Enron Corporation of Houston, was the son of a Baptist minister. "I was fully exposed to not only legal behavior," he says, "but moral and ethical behavior and what that means from the standpoint of leading organizations and people. I was, and am, a strong believer that one of the most satisfying things in life is to create a highly moral and ethical environment in which every individual is allowed and encouraged to realize their God-give potential."

John W. Rowe of New England Electric System speaks for many when he says that money is not what really motivates him. When a pastor in Maine came by to see him early in his career, he asked John how he liked his job. "It's important to value the business you're in and to take satisfaction from providing its services or good to others. At the end of the day, you want to respect what you do. In a certain sense, our work is us. We get into it, and it gets into us. . . . Business is about creating goods and services, jobs and benefits, and new wealth that didn't exist before."

John Rowe still remembers the stunned look on the minister's face when he said, "You mean you have a calling?"

Roger Sant was the Chairman and Dennis Bakke was the CEO of the AES Corporation, the global electricity company based in Arlington, Virginia. The company operates roughly ninety electricity plants in thirteen countries, employing some 40,000 people. They were interviewed in the *Harvard Business Review* in 1999. Bakke said, "When I give speeches nowadays and ask the audience, 'Why do businesses exist?' 75 percent of the people say the same thing. . . . They say, 'To make money.'"

"Capitalism is in great jeopardy if people hold on to that notion," he said. "Companies have to exist primarily in order to *contribute* to society, to meet its needs. Businesses have to help people live better lives. They have to operate in ways that help communities cohere and thrive."

"My belief in empowerment comes from my Christian faith," he says, "but many of my beliefs are not inconsistent with the fundamentals of Buddhism, Judaism, and Islam. I recently got a letter from an AES person who was leaving us to join a Buddhist monastery. She wrote, 'Thank you for giving me an opportunity to work in a company where I could fully live out my values.'

"We don't operate with the traditional notion that the company exists, first and foremost, for the benefit of the shareholders. Shareholders are one important constituency of our company, but they are not the most important. We have many other stakeholders: [employees], our customers, the communities we build and run our plants in, suppliers of debt and other services, and the governments of the countries where [we] operate."[36]

Not all businesses are divine callings. But many business ventures allow the opportunity for people to live out part of their vocational calling. My friend, Wilbur Stakes, is an example. Wilbur was a member of our church. His business was in international finance. One of his business partners is a member of the Ruling Family in Kuwait. Wilbur is a devout Christian and his partner is a devout Muslim, but their religious differences do not matter. They were speaking on the phone the other day, and his Muslim business partner said to him, "You are my brother, wherever we may go." What a wonderful statement of unquestioning trust and respect for the other person. That came not from studying the Bible or the Koran together, but from working together as business associates and fellow human beings.

I have talked to a number of business people over the years, inside and outside the church. Many of them have never been asked whether they regard what they do as a calling. They do not think about themselves that way. That has not been the language of the business schools, the economics textbooks, or the secularized speech of our time.

"But they could, and it would be better if they did," says Novak. "It would give them a greater sense of being part of a noble profession. It would raise their own esteem for what they do—and no doubt stimulate their imaginations about how they might gain greater and deeper satisfactions from doing it. . . . The human project is a universal project. We are involved in bringing the Creator's work to its intended fulfillment by being co-creators in a very grand project, indeed. . . . In particular, business has a special role to play in bringing hope—and actual economic progress—to the billion or so truly indigent people on this planet. . . . And that is one of the noblest callings inherent in business activities: to raise up the poor."[37]

I believe it is possible for a business person to look humbly, and

with pride, at their company's Annual Report, to look at the good
they have done for their employees and their families, for their
shareholders and their families, and for the earth and its families,
to whisper a prayer of thanks to God and to say with Paul, "Let
him who boasts, boast in the Lord."

God works through our work. Our work can become God's "love
made visible."

CHAPTER 9

LESSONS FROM THE TRAVELER'S WELCOME HOTEL

B. J. Stone runs the Livery in the God-forsaken town of Twenty-Mile. Together with his helper, Coots, they take care of the half-dead donkeys that are used in the mine shafts. Mr. Kane owns the Mercantile Emporium. The Bjorkvists run the Boardinghouse which caters to the miners on the weekends, after they have checked into the Traveler's Welcome Hotel (which is not really a hotel, but a place for the "working girls" to practice their trade). They are all characters in a historical novel called, *Incident at Twenty-Mile* by Trevanian, one of my favorite writers.

In one of his lectures to his young friend, Matthew, the self-taught teacher B. J. Stone says, "There are two things in this life that are easily squandered, and too late regretted: time and friends. The wise man either spends his time well or wastes it gracefully. But he never, never lets a friendship shrivel and die for lack of attention. Friendships are just too precious. Too rare. Too fragile."

When young Matthew tells Stone not to worry because he has plenty of friends, like the girls in the Traveler's Welcome Hotel, B.J. says, "Sentiment is to love what ethics are to morality, or what legality is to justice, or justice is to compassion—all degraded forms of a loftier ideal."[38]

The final word of the battle cry of the French Revolution has always rung strange to most of us Americans. We understand "Liberty and Equality." But what is this "Fraternity"? Why would revolutionaries value it as something to be fought for with the same passion as liberty and equality?

I would define fraternity as an affection or love that binds members of a group together. When I use the word "love" here, what I mean is that fraternal kind of love, a brother-to-brother, sister-to-sister, sister-to-brother love. If we do not have that, all our other values are degraded forms of a loftier ideal.

The highest expression of this kind of fraternal love in the ancient world was the Ten Commandments—the Ten Words of God. But that wasn't enough. The ten soon became 547, and then thousands more lesser laws were added to clarify those.

Law multiplies. Love expands. Jesus reduced the Law to its loftier ideal, and thereby expanded its demands. He told us that the Ten Commandments and all of the other laws in the Bible can be summarized in two: "Love your God and Love your Neighbor." Law can help protect us, but it cannot save us. Only Love can do that.

My friend and mentor-in-truth, Bill Coffin, often reminded us that there are four major ethical stages in history. The first is *unlimited retaliation*. "Most people shudder when they hear 'an eye for an eye' and 'a tooth for a tooth.' But far from commanding revenge, the law insists that a person must never take more than one eye for an eye, never more than one tooth for a tooth. This law in the Book of Exodus became necessary to guard against the normal way people had of doing business . . .: 'Kill my cat and I'll kill yours, your dog, your mule, and you, too' [Exodus 21:24]. The father/mother of unlimited retaliation is, of course, the notion that might makes right, an uncivilized concept if ever there was one, that to this day governs the actions of many so-called civilized nations.

"The second stage, *limited retaliation*, is certainly an improvement over unlimited retaliation: 'Get even, but no more.' Limited retaliation is what most people have in mind when they speak of criminal justice—'You did the crime, you do the time.' Limited retaliation is also the justification most frequently used for capital punishment, the most premeditated form of killing in the world." And of all the enlightened nations of the world, ours is the only one to practice it.

"Unlimited retaliation, limited retaliation. A third stage might be called *limited love*. In Leviticus 19:18 it is written: 'You shall not take vengeance nor bear a grudge against the children of your own people, but you shall love your neighbor as yourself.'

"Again, a step forward. Limited love is better than limited retaliation, and limited love can be very moving—a mother's love for her child, children's love for their parents. But when the neighbor to be loved has been limited to one of one's own people, then lim-

ited love, historically, has supported White supremacy, religious
bigotry [pogroms] . . . and 'America for Americans' (which never
included Native Americans).

"Jesus, of course, was pressing for a fourth state, *unlimited love*,
the love that is of God, the love you give when you make a gift of
yourself, no preconditions. (Have you ever noticed how Jesus
healed with no strings attached? He didn't say to blind Bartimeus,
now healed, 'Now don't you go ogling beautiful women.' To the
owner of the withered hand he restored, Jesus didn't warn, 'No
stealing now.') And the neighbor to be loved, according to the
parable of the Good Samaritan, is the nearest person in need
regardless of race, religion, or nationality, and we can safely add
gender or sexual orientation."[39]

This is the love God wants from us: not *unlimited retaliation*, nor
limited retaliation, nor even *limited love*, but *unlimited love*. And
unlimited love can only come from God's gift of a new heart and
a new spirit.

Marriage is a fraternal metaphor used by God to explain his new
relationship with Hosea and those who had formerly worshipped
Baal:

> "And I will betroth you to me for ever;
> and I will betroth you to me in righteousness
>   and in justice,
> in steadfast love and in compassion.
> And I will betroth you to me in faithfulness,
> And you shall know the Lord."[40]

Familial honor for other human beings cannot be legislated. It
is an attitude of the human heart.

Old B. J. Stone had it right: "There are two things in this life that
are easily squandered, and too late regretted: time and friends. The
wise man either spends his time well or wastes it gracefully. But he
never, never lets a friendship shrivel and die for lack of attention."

LOTS OF
LOVE . . .
FOR
CHRISTMAS

CHAPTER 10

THE SMALLEST PACKAGE IN THE WORLD

There you are, stalking the malls, walking the aisles, searching for that extra-special gift. Stashing away a few dollars a month to buy him that jazzy computer; staring at a thousand rings to find her the best diamond; staying up all night Christmas Eve assembling the new bicycle.

Why do you do it? You do it so that their eyes will pop, their jaw will drop. You do it to hear those words of disbelief: "You did this for me?!" That's why most of us give to others—to see and feel their astonishment at being loved.

As William Sloane Coffin put it, "Love measures our stature: the more we love, the bigger we are. *There is no smaller package in the world than that of a person all wrapped up in themself!"*

Thomas Merton, the modern day saint, put it precisely: "Love is our true destiny. We do not find the meaning of life by ourselves alone—we find it with another. We do not discover the secret of our lives merely by study and calculation in our own isolated meditations. The meaning of our life is a secret that has to be revealed to us in love, *by the one we love*. And if this love is unreal, the secret will not be found, the meaning will never reveal itself, the message will never be decoded. . . . *The person who loves is more alive and more real than they were when they did not love."*

Will Ross tells of being with his wife at the Baltimore Airport on October 27, 2007. His flight had been cancelled because of the California fires. "When I went to check in at the United counter [the next morning]," he says, "I saw a lot of soldiers home from Iraq. Most were young and all had on their desert camouflage uniforms. . . . It was a visible reminder that we are in a war. It probably was pretty close to what train terminals were like in World War II.

"Many people were stopping the troops to talk to them or just say, 'Welcome Home.' Because the weather was so terrible and the flights were backed up, there were a lot of unhappy people in the terminal trying to get home, but nobody that I saw gave the soldiers a hard time.

"By the afternoon, one plane to Denver had been delayed several hours. United Airlines personnel kept asking for volunteers to give-up their seats and take another flight. They weren't getting many volunteers.

"Finally a United spokeswoman got on the PA and said, 'Folks, as you can see, there are a lot of soldiers in the waiting area. They only have 14 days of leave, and we're trying to get them where they need to go without spending any more time in an airport than they have to. We sold them all tickets, knowing we would oversell the flight. If we can, we want to get them all on this flight. We want all the soldiers to know that we respect what you're doing, we are here for you, and we love you.'

"At that, the entire terminal of cranky, tired, travel-weary people, a cross-section of America, broke into sustained and heartfelt applause. The soldiers looked surprised and very modest. Most of them just looked at their boots. Many of us were wiping away tears.

"And, yes, people lined up to take the later flight and all the soldiers went to Denver on that flight. That little moment made me proud to be an American."

That afternoon in an airport in Baltimore, some eyes popped, some jaws dropped, and some soldiers with tears in their eyes said, *"You did this for me?"*

And a grateful nation on Christmas Eve, hanging their stockings by the fire with care and in safety because of their sacrifice, responds, *"You bet! You did this for us. We can do no less."*

The true miracle of Christmas takes place every moment in the Bethlehems of our hearts. "Everything we are or have is freely given by the God of love. All is grace. Light and water, shelter and food, work and free time, children, parents, grandparents, life and death—it is all given to us. Why? So that we can say thanks: thanks to God, thanks to each other, thanks to all and everyone." (Henri Nouwen)

> "There is no difficulty that enough love will not conquer;
> no disease that enough love will not heal;

no door that enough love will not open;
no gulf that enough love will not bridge;
no wall that enough love will not throw down;
no sin that enough love will not redeem."
—Emmet Fox

"The Christian hope we celebrate this Christmas Eve must be seen as an ultimate optimism which takes into account all of the evil and sorrow which make people tend toward pessimism. That almost every inch of the earth's surface [has been] soaked today with the tears and the blood of innocents is not God's fault, it is our own."

And since we humans created it, we can eradicate it. No matter how dark the night, the Christ will be born at midnight.

War is not inevitable; fear is not inevitable; fractured families and relationships are not inevitable; hopelessness is not inevitable.

As my South African friend, Dr. Alan Maker, puts it, "At the center of the universe this Christmas Eve is a *Heartbeat of Love*. It is incredible and inaudible. Our task is to get close enough to that heartbeat to make it credible and audible by our words and deeds. . . ."

And to affirm with our lives:

that love is stronger than hate,
that the power to heal is greater than the power to destroy,
that the power of sharing is stronger than the power of greed,
and that the power of love is greater than the power of despair.

The birth of Christ is the birth of Love.

"You did this for me? Why did you do it?" we may well ask of God this Christmas Eve. *"Why did you go to all that trouble?"*

"Why," says God. *"I did it so that your eyes would pop, your jaws would drop . . . Do you like it? I did it just for you!"*

CHAPTER 11

DON'T GIVE UP
ON LOVE

At least we can be grateful to the merchandising industry for keeping alive the Christmas Spirit, even for those of us live in a snowless clime. I was struck with the recent advertisement for Lladro statuary. Their ad shows a humble manger scene with this sentiment: *"A Tradition to Cherish. Purchase Baby Jesus, Mary and St. Joseph and receive this attractive stable as our gift to you."* As if that weren't enough, the small print promises, *"Peace of Mind with the Lladro Assurance Program."* Well, there you have it. What more could you want? . . . Peace of Mind *and* an attractive stable! All this can be yours just for purchasing Jesus!

I am reminded of the timeless adage, "People are to Love. Things are to Use. Don't get the two confused."

A little boy was sprawled out on the floor working hard on a drawing when his daddy asked him what he was doing. The reply came back, "Drawing a picture of God." His daddy said, "You can't do that, honey. Nobody knows what God looks like." But the little boy continued to draw and said very matter-of-factly, "They will in a few minutes."

That is the true message of Christmas. Nobody knew then what God truly looked like until Jesus. And nobody will know what God looks like now until you and I draw a similar picture with our own lives.

I say it again: At the center of the universe is a heartbeat of love—invisible and incredible. Our job is to get close enough to that heartbeat that it beats through us and becomes visible and credible in us.

As the thirteenth-century German mystic and heretic, Meister Eckhart, wrote:

> *What good . . . this birth?*
> *What good is it to me*
> *If this eternal birth of the divine Son*
> *Takes place unceasingly*
> *But does not take place*
> *Within myself?*

And what good is it to me
If Mary is full of grace
if I am not also full of grace?
What good is it to me
For the Creator to bring forth this Holy Child
If the Child is not also born in me
In my time
And in my culture?
This, then, is the fullness of time:
When the Son of God
Is begotten
In us."

In Hebrew, *"immanu"* means "with us" and *"El"* is the short form for "God"—*"Immanuel,"* "God with Us." The point of Matthew's allusion to the miraculous conception of Jesus is not to describe Jesus's *essential nature*, as the Greeks did with their demigods (half human by virtue of birth from a human mother, and half divine by virtue of having been begotten by a god). No. This is a Jewish, not a Greek story. Its purpose is to describe Jesus's *function* as the one who has a major role to play in God's drama of salvation. Mary represents Isaiah's prophecy of Virgin Israel, who cannot bring forth the Messiah without God's direct intervention.[41]

What is it in the Christmas Story of Jesus that drives us to say, "God was in that life"? There is something expansive and creative in the boundary-breaking love that we meet in the life of Jesus. When we humans know love, we seem to grow; without love we die.

As Bishop John Spong puts it in his book, *A New Christianity for a New World*, "Love is manifested in the human willingness to venture beyond the boundaries of safety, to risk losing ourselves, and even in the desire to explore the crevices of the unknown. Love creates stability, but not stagnation. Love calls us into being; it expands our lives as it flows through us. If love is ever blocked, it dies. Love has to be shared, or it ceases to be love. Love binds us

into larger and larger communities. Love frees us from the pejorative definitions that result in exclusion. Love transcends barriers,
unites and calls. Love enhances life.

"So when a human being appears in history with a greater ability to love than we have ever knowingly witnessed before, when
this life calls us into a new human unity and refuses to be bound
by the rules that rise out of our incompleteness and our fear, then
we inevitably look at that life with awe, perhaps even with
worship. . . . Love has no chosen people, for that implies that some
are unchosen. Love bears no malice, seeks no revenge, guards no
doorway.

"A life defined by love will not seek to protect itself or to justify
itself. It will be content simply to be itself and to give itself away
with abandon. If denied, love embraces the denier. If betrayed, love
embraces the betrayer. If forsaken, love embraces the forsaker. If
tortured, love embraces the torturer. If crucified, love embraces the
killers. Love never judges. Love simply announces that neither the
person you are, nor the deeds you have done, have erected a barrier which the power of this invincible presence cannot overcome.

"Love lifts us beyond our quest for survival. Love enables us to
transcend our limits. Love frees us to give ourselves away. . . . I call
that love 'God.' I see it in Jesus of Nazareth, and I find myself called
into a new being, a boundary-free humanity, and made whole in
its presence. So *God was in Christ*, I say. Jesus thus reveals the source
of love, and then he calls us to enter it."[42]

Two days after terrorists unleashed their world-shaking assault
on the World Trade Towers and the Pentagon in 2001, there was
another shaking of the world. Connecticut Senator Chris Dodd's
world changed forever when he became a father for the first time,
at 57 years of age. His wife Jackie gave birth to their daughter,
Grace. ("We thought that week the world could use a little Grace,"
he said.) Within minutes of her arrival, the two doctors and pedi-
atric nurse attending her revealed they were natives of Afghan-
istan, Iran, and Lebanon. "The first hands to hold this wonderful
daughter of mine," Chris said, "were from that part of the world.

. . . The first hands to have really held her, washed her and cleaned her were these three people. What a bright light it was at this spot in the midst of all this."

In an emotional floor speech the day after the attacks, but the day before Grace's birth, Senator Dodd told his colleagues, "I want to end on this note and say to [those Senators who have just had babies, and to] my unborn child that we are going to build a world for you that is deserving of the kind of place you ought to have. Previous generations did it for us," he said. "We commit to you that you will live in a peaceful world. That is our common goal."[43]

How can that tiny infant boy whom Joseph held in one hand change the world? How could that tiny infant girl whom Chris Dodd held in one hand change the world? Because God's love is visionary. It does not seek love; it creates it. Because, as Carl Sandburg wrote, "There is only one child in the world; and the child's name is ALL CHILDREN." Every child is our child, and the answer to children's suffering begins with each of us. Either we put an end to war, or war will put an end to us.

"He became like us, that we might become like him," it has been said of Jesus. When the world realizes that, then our children shall not be robbed of their inheritance. That, my readers, is the Christmas message. Divine love has come to us again, just as it has for centuries, wrapped up in human flesh: his and ours.

In this loud season of fear, sorrow, and loss, we wait for that cosmic whimper—the sound of a baby cooing, stirring, crying. At the outskirts of our awareness is this wee one, our brother, our sister, made of the same stuff as the children all around us. In that distinct whimpering of Love is our Hope, and the Hope of the world.

> "Yea, Lord, we greet Thee
> Born this happy morning,
> Jesus, to Thee be all glory given;
> Word of the Father,
> Now in flesh appearing!
> O come, let us adore Him . . .
> Christ, the Lord."[44]

CHAPTER 12

GOD LOVES THE WHOLE WORLD— NO EXCEPTIONS

" . . . and they shall name him 'Emmanuel,'
which means, 'God is with us.'"
—MATTHEW 1:23

"**G**od is with us." Quite a stretch of imagination for two peasant teenagers in trouble! But they seemed to believe it. And so do we. I love the recklessness of faith . . . first you leap, and then you grow wings.

As they say, "the Bible is true . . . and some things happened!" So let's not throw the baby Jesus out with the bathwater of bad religion.

I was taken aback in 2006 when I read the following large Christmas ad for Richard Dawkins' recently published book:

> "This Christmas Imagine: NO RELIGION!
> No Crusades
> No Inquisition
> No Pogroms
> No 9/11
> No Suicide Bombings!
>
> This holiday, give the national bestseller, *The God Delusion.*
> 'Everyone should read it!'"

Dawkins is a widely recognized British evolutionary biologist and atheist who retired from Oxford in 2008. His scathing critique of organized religion reached #4 on the *New York Times* Best-Seller list and remained on the list for 51 weeks.

Dawkin's message is essentially that to be an atheist is a "brave and splendid" aspiration. Belief in God is not only a delusion, he argues, but a "pernicious" one. "I cannot know for certain," he says, "but I think God is very improbable, and I live my life on the assumption that he is not there."

Well, as a committed Christian, I live in the same world that Dawkins does. I see the same cruelty and caring. I have the same heart throbs and heartbreaks. But I come to the opposite conclusion. My experience leads me to believe that not just the world, but in fact the entire universe, is "in God"—while at the same time "God is within" every atom, every molecule, and DNA of the universe. I live my life on the assumption that God *is* there.

We are, as they say, poised on the horns of a dilemma. And the worst thing one can do with a dilemma is to resolve it prematurely because we haven't the courage to live with uncertainty. I do agree with Dawkins that religion can be, and has been, a cruel and terrible thing. Throughout history more people have been killed in the name of religion than any other cause. Religious intolerance is one of the prime causes of hatred, war, and terrorism.

In his book, *The Origins of Unbelief in America*, James Turner goes so far as to say: "Unbelief was not something that 'happened' to religion. On the contrary, religion caused unbelief."[45]

As Mark Twain wrote, "So much blood has been shed by the Church because of an omission from the Gospel: 'Ye shall be indifferent as to what your neighbor's religion is.' Not merely tolerant of it, but indifferent to it. Divinity is claimed for many religions; but no religion is great enough or divine enough to add that new law to its code."[46]

The great evil of our day is not our separate religions. The real problem is that *we just do not like each other*. "The Other," the "One Different from Ourselves" is despised. The Other is feared and hated. I believe this single motive is at the heart of every crusade, every inquisition, every pogrom, every terrorist attack like 9/11, and every suicide bombing. We just don't like one another. Add an intolerant religious absolutism to this deep distrust and hatred of those who are different from us, and you have this terrible ratcheting of violence we see increasing every day around the world.

Yet we have the audacity during the Christmas season to sing of the birth and reign of the Prince of Peace. Christmas celebrates what theologians like to call the "in-carnation," the "en-flesh-ment" of God, the time when God's love appears on the earth in human form—"Word of the Father, now in flesh appearing." But the Incarnation is not just about Jesus! Christmas is not just about what *God* has become, but what *we* are to become. Christ became like us so that we might become like him. "He comes to convert us, not from life to something more than life, but rather from something less than life to the possibility of full life itself."[47]

As Ireneus, the early Christian Father, translated it: "The glory of God is a human being fully alive." The point here is that each of us can birth God into the world. We can each become like Mary —*theotokis*—"God-bearers."

God is bigger than any of our ideas about God. No one person nor one religion or creed has absolute claims on the truth. God's love and justice is for all people, so it takes different forms at different times in different cultures.

For many of us, God is defined by Jesus, but God is not confined to Jesus. Believing in Jesus does not mean believing doctrines about him. Rather, it means to give one's heart, one's self at its deepest level, to the living Lord, and then to attempt to follow Jesus's lead in our actions.

My editorialist friend, Mike Turpin, a member of my former church in Connecticut, put it this way:

"If I want my family to develop skills to cope in a world that seems so unwilling to reward character over charisma, they will need some spiritual grounding and it's up to my wife and me to ensure this happens. The key was finding a church home that felt right. . . . We sought a church that offered a community of people that sought to understand before being understood. [Our church] preaches tolerance, inclusion and responsibility to be a peacemaker. [We] avoid the harder edges of a more orthodox theology that can sometimes judge, exclude, or seek to proselytize those who do not exactly blend into a singular view. My Catholic, Jewish, Mormon, Islamic and Hindu friends all have found similar experiences . . . as they sought a community that helped them form a healthier spiritual balance in life."[48]

Long before that Holy Night, when God's love was born into this world, the spirit of Christmas was at work in the world—in the lives of children, teenagers, and adults—just as it is today . . .

> wherever peace is cobbled together out of the
> broken fragments of relationships . . .

wherever human beings reach out to build better lives
for everyone . . .
wherever people preach or teach or embody ways in
which the Continuous Creator of heaven and earth
loves us, empowers us, and will never let us go . . .
there is God alive in our midst.

Diversity may well be both the hardest thing to live with and
the most dangerous thing to be without. As Christians, you and I
can sing our "Alleluias" to God and our love for Jesus without
denying others access to that same God through a different way.

Ours is a faith that embraces ambiguity and that honors
other faiths . . .
a faith that builds bridges, not walls, between people . . .
a faith that binds strangers together with love and
affection, not with rules and guilt . . .
and a faith that insists that basic human values be
embodied in the social order of our nation.

When that happens, "A new day will be formed, and Jesus—
who crossed every boundary of tribe, prejudice, gender and religion—will be honored by [all] those who, as his disciples, have
transcended the boundaries of even the religious system that was
created to honor him."[49]

On the final page of his classic tale, *A Christmas Carol*, Charles
Dickens has Tiny Tim Cratchit leaning forward on his crutches
with a huge smile on his face, announcing to his family, "God
Bless Us, Every One."

I want us to carry that announcement a step further . . .

"God Bless the Whole World—NO EXCEPTIONS!"

CHAPTER 13

DIAMONDS IN
THE NIGHT

At exactly 11:45 PM the chimes began ringing, signaling the final minutes of the life of Ebeneezer Scrooge. "Forgive me if I am not justified in what I ask," said Scrooge, looking intently at the [Second] Spirit's robe, "but I see something strange, and not belonging to yourself, protruding from your skirts. Is it a foot or a claw!"

"It might be a claw, for the flesh there is upon it," was the Spirit's sorrowful reply. "Look here."

From the foldings of its robe, it brought two children; wretched, abject, frightful, hideous, miserable. They knelt down at its feet, and clung upon the outside of its garment. . . . They were a boy and girl.

"Spirit! Are they yours?" Scrooge could say no more.

"They are Man's," said the Spirit, looking down upon them. "This boy is Ignorance. This girl is Want."

"Have they no refuge or resource?" cried Scrooge.

"Are there no prisons?" said the Spirit, turning on him for the last time with his own words. "Are there no workhouses?"

[Then] the bell struck twelve.[50]

In his Preface to *A Christmas Carol*, Charles Dickens wishes the reader, "May it haunt [your] houses pleasantly. . . ." And so it has since it was first published in 1843!

Dickens knew whereof he spoke. He was not simply a marvelous storyteller; he was one of the most influential social reformers of England's nineteenth century—which abolished debtor prison, improved conditions of child labor, and cleansed the English schools of their worst disciplinary barbarities.

What made him so effective was that he had suffered from those same abominations. Micawber, Dickens's father, had been in a debtor's prison. As a young boy, crushed with shame and crippled with poverty, Dickens had gone up to the depressing prison day after day to visit him. When ten years old, he worked long hours for a pittance pasting labels on bottles in a blacking factory and endured the cruelties of an old school system.

There is an old saying: "When fate throws a dagger at you, there are two ways to catch it: either by the blade or by the handle. Catch the dagger by the blade and it may cut you, perhaps kill you. But if you catch it by the handle, you can use it to fight your way through whatever it is that you are dealing with." That is the power of *A Christmas Carol* and of a manger.

Harry Emerson Fosdick, the great preacher of New York City's Riverside Church, recounted the story of a friend who was visiting the state of Maine. He came upon an apple tree so loaded with fruit that the laden branches were propped to keep them from the ground. When the friend inquired about it, the owner of the orchard said, "Go look at that tree's trunk near the bottom."

His friend went and examined it and discovered that the tree had been badly wounded with a deep gash. "That's something we learned about apple trees," said the owner of the orchard. "When the trees tend to run to wood and leaves and not to fruit, we wound it and gash it, and almost always, no one knows why, this is the result: it turns its energies into fruit."

As a pastor, I know that these have not been the best of years for many. In the midst of a fluctuating economy, some have lost their jobs. In the midst of celebrations of new birth, some have lost their dearest loved ones. In the midst of exciting change in a new world of ever-expanding possibilities, some have mourned the loss of a world they once knew and loved and in which they felt safe.

Still, I believe that hope has not died—that the light has become brighter—that there is a new world of life for each of us, and all the world, waiting to be discovered. A storyteller saw that dream and made it a reality of hope in the slums of old England. A gardener saw that dream and made it a reality of abundant fruit from a gashed and wounded tree. As awful and as undeserving as adversity can be, it can flush out of people tremendous virtue. The unfairness of life can stimulate passions and strengths never known before.

When the Royal Palace in Tehran, Iran, was being built, the architect sent an order for mirrors to cover the entrance walls. Just as the palace was about to be completed, the mirrors finally arrived in huge crates. The workers took the crates apart and, to their dismay, all they found were broken pieces of mirrors. They were all smashed in transit. The architect, as you might imagine, was depressed.

The whole construction crew was at a standstill until the architect came up with a brilliant idea. He took the broken pieces of mirror and began to fit them onto the entrance wall, one piece at a time, as though he were constructing a mosaic. The end result was an entranceway that would take your breath away. The entranceway looks as though it's covered with diamonds. The broken pieces of mirror produce a crystal effect, throwing out the colors of the rainbow on all who pass by them.

Your hearts may have been broken this past year, your lives may have been devastated, your hopes may have been shattered. But you and I can choose to pick up the pieces, to gather up the broken parts of our heart, and from the rubble, reconstruct a new and beautiful life.

A babe in a manger of straw is all that it took to bring down the powerful forces of darkness and reconstruct a society of hate into a society of love. Once again as we near Christmas, the labor pains of love are almost over. Life and light are being born in darkness even now. The candle which has dispelled two thousand years of sorrow is brighter now than ever before. Its light will spread throughout the world and the fragments of shattered mirrors will reflect the brilliance of a thousand diamonds in the night.

> *For unto us a Child is born,*
> *unto us a Son is given . . .*
> *and his name shall be called*
> *"Wonderful Counselor, Almighty God,*
> *Everlasting Father, the Prince of Peace."*
> —ISAIAH 9:6

CHAPTER 14

YES, VIRGINIA, THERE IS A CHRIST CHILD

In September, 1897, a young girl from New York was laughed at and made fun of by her school friends because she told them she believed in Santa Claus. She asked her father if he believed, but he was not very helpful. So, she wrote to the highest authority she could think of, which was the *The New York Sun* newspaper.

"I am 8 years old," she wrote. "Some of my little friends say there is no Santa Claus. Papa says, 'If you see it in The Sun, *it's so.' Please tell me the truth, is there a Santa Claus?"*—SIGNED, VIRGINIA O'HANLON

Her letter found its way into the hands of a veteran editor, Francis P. Church, the son of a Baptist minister. Church had covered the Civil War for *The New York Times* and was given the controversial assignments on the editorial page. Mr. Church knew that there was no avoiding the question and that he must answer truthfully. So he turned to his desk, and began his reply which was to become one of the most memorable editorials in newspaper history.

"Virginia, your little friends are wrong. They have been affected by the skepticism of a skeptical age. They do not believe except they see. They think that nothing can be which is not comprehensible by their little minds. All minds, Virginia, whether they be men's or children's, are little. In this great universe of ours, man is a mere insect, an ant, in his intellect as compared with the boundless world about him, as measured by the intelligence capable of grasping the whole of truth and knowledge.

"Yes, Virginia, there is a Santa Claus.

"He exists as certainly as love and generosity and devotion exist, and you know that they abound and give to your life its highest beauty and joy. Alas! how dreary would be the world if there were no Santa Claus! It would be as dreary as if there were no Virginias. There would be no childlike faith then, no poetry, no romance to make tolerable this existence. We should have no enjoyment, except in sense and sight. The external light with which childhood fills the world would be extinguished.

"Not believe in Santa Claus! You might as well not believe in fairies. . . . Did you ever see fairies dancing on the lawn? Of course not, but that's no proof that they are not there. Nobody can conceive or imagine all the wonders there are unseen and unseeable in the world.

"You tear apart the baby's rattle and see what makes the noise inside, but there is a veil covering the unseen world which not the strongest man, nor even the united strength of all the strongest men that ever lived could tear apart. Only faith, poetry, love, romance, can push aside that curtain and view and picture the supernatural beauty and glory beyond. Is it all real? Ah, Virginia, in all this world there is nothing else real and abiding.

"No Santa Claus? Thank God he lives and lives forever. A thousand years from now, Virginia, nay 10 times 10,000 years from now, he will continue to make glad the heart of childhood."

Merry Christmas and a Happy New Year!!!!

Virginia went on to be a public school teacher and principal. Her letter was printed in *The Sun* every year until 1949, when the paper went out of business. She received a steady stream of mail from readers until she died in 1971.

English writer Graham Greene once ended a short story by calling a dying man's affectionate gesture "only one more indication of a human being's capacity for self-deception, our baseless optimism that is so much more appalling than our despair."

Yet 108 years ago, an eight-year-old girl's question shamed the cynical pessimism of generations of so-called "educated" adults.

I suggest to you that Virginia's question may be different today. With the welcome openness of our times in which scholars and others scrutinize the Bible and the Christian religion through the lenses of history, culture, and the scientific method, there are those who question the ancient story. As well they should.

So we are right to ask, with Virginia, "Please tell me the truth, is there a Christ Child?" And I suggest to you on Christmas Eve that the church's answer to its modern critics is the same as Francis

Church's answer to Virginia's question so long ago.

As Bill Coffin put it, "Every Christmas I'm struck at how the Word of the Lord hits the world with the force of a hint. We want God to be GOD, and God wants to be a babe in a manger."

". . . Christmas itself is by grace. It could never have survived our blindness and [plundering] otherwise. It could never have happened otherwise. Perhaps it is the very wildness and strangeness of the grace that has led us to try to tame it. We have tried to make it habitable. We have roofed it in and furnished it. We have reduced it to an occasion we feel at home with, at best a touching and beautiful occasion, at worst a trite one. But if the Christmas event is indeed—as a matter of cold, hard fact—all it's cracked up to be, then even our best efforts are misleading."[51]

There is "a veil covering the unseen world" which "only faith, poetry, love, and romance can push aside." And, as Charles Dickens put it, "In [this] season of immortal HOPE and on the birthday of immortal MERCY, we will shut out NOTHING."

What is Christmas?

> *"It is the rainbow arched over the roof of the sky when the clouds*
> *are heavy with foreboding.*
> *It is the cry of life in the newborn babe when, forced from its*
> *mother's nest, it claims its right to live.*
> *It is the brooding Presence of the Eternal Spirit making crooked*
> *paths straight, rough places smooth, tired hearts refreshed,*
> *dead hopes stirred with the newness of life.*
> *It is the promise of tomorrow at the close of every day,*
> *the movement of life in defiance of death,*
> *and the assurance that love is sturdier than hate,*
> *that right is more confident than wrong,*
> *that good is more permanent than evil."*[52]

"Yes, Virginia, there is a Christ Child." In all of this world, there is nothing else real and abiding. Thank God he lives and lives forever. **Amen.**

CHAPTER 15

PAYING IT FORWARD
AT CHRISTMAS

On the first day of school, the seventh graders are shocked when their social studies teacher writes the year's assignment on the blackboard: "Think of an idea that could change the world."

Their teacher is not much of an optimist himself. His face is scarred with burns. What he has seen of the world has given him a cold intensity. He doesn't really expect his students to shake off their adolescent lethargy. But he is not about to coddle them either.

One boy takes him up on his challenge. Trevor McKinney proposes a chain letter of good deeds. He'll do a good deed for three people (it has to be something important and something hard, he says), and then he will instruct each recipient to pay him back by "paying it forward" to someone else. Someone does you a good turn. You pass it on to three other people. They pass it on, and so on.

His teacher tells him that he thinks his idea is a bit "Utopian." So Trevor looks up the word in a dictionary and replies, "What's wrong with that?" Trevor is a resourceful latchkey kid whose father has disappeared and whose mother is a recovering alcoholic working two jobs, one of them as a waitress in a Las Vegas strip joint. So Trevor puts his idea into practice by inviting a homeless man to establish residency in his garage—without telling his mother!

Well, no good deed goes unpunished, as they say. Trevor's act of compassion is regarded as socially outrageous by his classmates, and ludicrous by his mother, who heads off to school to scold his teacher. Every person Trevor tries to help ends up back where they were before, or worse. Finally, just as he is about to give up, his plan begins to take root and blossom.

As Trevor discovers, "paying it forward" does work if you want to change something bad enough that needs fixing. . . . As he says, "If it's hard to do . . . and if it's not planned—you have to be watching" for the right person and the right moment. As anyone who has been in Alcoholics Anonymous knows, paying it forward is the Twelfth Step.

Film critic Roger Ebert thinks that *Pay it Forward* is a naïve movie. "It's a seductive theory," he says, "but in the real world, altruism is less powerful than selfishness, greed, nepotism, xenophobia, tribalism and paranoia. If you doubt me, take another look at the front pages [of our newspapers]."[53]

I am glad that I don't agree with Roger Ebert. Love and generosity can change the world. In fact, in the end, they are the only things that can. Truth may be buried for a while, but Truth will rise again. If the landfills of disposable Christmas presents across our land teach us anything, it is that there is no true happiness in getting or in having, but only in giving that which cannot be taken away.

As any mother knows, "paying it forward" is worth the cost. Mary and her cousin Elizabeth were no exceptions. Both were pregnant. Both were excited and joyful, 'though for Mary, the excitement was tempered with fear and anxiety. For both mothers-to-be, their pregnancies were a time of waiting, of hope, and of ultimate sacrifice.

"In the end," writes Kathy Coffey, "they will remember their nine-month 'confinement' as nothing, their painful labor as hardly worth talking about. Every loss fades into the light of this gain, this precious and irreplaceable child. For [each of them], life's center has shifted, from her own hopes and dreams to those of the child in her womb. For both [of them], God has touched their lives in the child within them."[54]

That is what Christmas is all about: Embracing the joy and fulfillment that can be found only in finding God in others, embracing suffering and pain and hard work as the only path to building a life worth living, and a life that goes on living after us.

As St. Augustine preached: "God loved us so much that [the One] who made time entered time for our sake; [the One] who is an eternity older than the world became younger in the world than many of his servants; [the One] who made humanity became human. God became a creature through a mother God had created, God was carried in arms God made, God nursed at breasts God had formed. From God's crib arose in his infant cries the Word of God, without whom all human eloquence falls mute."

Christmas is all about God "paying it forward" in us. Christmas is about the birth of Christ—in us. The story of Jesus's conception by the Spirit describes how it always happens: Christ is born in us through the union of the Spirit of God with our flesh. Clearly, it was a risk of spontaneous, gracious generosity for God to have "paid it forward" in giving us birth in the first place. Then God outdid God's self a second time in giving us God's very self in Jesus. Now God gives us the wondrous opportunity to "birth ourselves" in others.

When I was a child, I thought Christmas was about something that happened once upon a time. Now I see that Christmas is about what happens again and again and again. "Christ in you [and in me], the hope of glory."[55]

We are all "mothers of God." For God is always needing to be born.[56]

Listen to how Ann Weems catches this in her poem, "Christmas Comes":

> *Christmas comes every time we see God in other persons.*
> *The human and the holy meet in Bethlehem*
>   *or in Times Square,*
> *For Christmas comes like a golden storm on its way*
>   *to Jerusalem—*
> *Determinedly, inevitably . . .*
>
> *Even Now it comes*
> *In the face of hatred and warring—*
>   *No atrocity too terrible to stop it,*
>   *No Herod strong enough,*
>   *No hurt deep enough,*
>   *No curse shocking enough,*
>   *No disaster shattering enough.*

For someone on earth will see the star,
   Someone will hear the angel voices,
   Someone will run to Bethlehem,
   Someone will know peace and goodwill:
   The Christ will be born![57]

And so in the place where you are this day, "Let every heart prepare him room. . . . And heaven and nature sing!"[58]

CHAPTER 16

THE OUTRAGE
OF LIGHT

This year in particular, the light of Christmas candles is set against the darkness of terror and war. In nights like these, the mere presence of light is a statement of outrage against the darkness. Everywhere on earth, it seems, there is a rising darkness—killing God's children in the name of God. Where is the Peace on Earth the angels proclaimed so long ago?

One is reminded of the heavenly vision of George Fox, founder of the Society of Friends:

> *"And I saw that there was an*
> *Ocean of Darkness and Death;" he writes,*
> *"But an infinite*
> *Ocean of Light and Love*
> *flowed over the Ocean of Darkness;*
> *and in that I saw the*
> *infinite love of God.*

Almost 150 years ago, during our nation's Civil War, which claimed 600,000 lives, the events of history felt as dark as they do today. For four years the North and the South fought a war that proved to be one of the bloodiest in history, tearing apart the country, families, and friends.

In 1863, the poet Henry Wadsworth Longfellow wrote a poem called, "Christmas Bells," at a time of personal dejection over the Civil War and the loss of his second wife, Fanny, who died of burns during a freak accident in their Cambridge home. When Longfellow tried to save her, he suffered burns on his hands and face, which scarred him for life. The man who seemed to be a perennial optimist understood the darkness of pessimism, and he wrote this poem as a statement on despair and hope:

> *"I heard the bells on Christmas Day*
> *Their old, familiar carols play,*
> *And wild and sweet*
> *The words repeat*
> *Of peace on earth, good-will to men!*

And thought how, as the day had come,
*   The belfries of all Christendom*
*   Had rolled along*
The unbroken song
Of peace on earth, good-will to men!

Till ringing, singing on its way,
The world revolved from night to day,
*   A voice, a chime,*
*   A chant sublime*
Of peace on earth, good-will to men!

Then from each black, accursed mouth
The cannon thundered in the South,
*   And with the sound*
*   The carols drowned*
Of peace on earth, good-will to men!

It was as if an earthquake rent
The hearth-stones of a continent,
*   And made forlorn*
*   The households born*
Of peace on earth, good-will to men!

And in despair I bowed my head;
"There is no peace on earth," I said;
*   "For hate is strong,*
*   And mocks the song*
Of peace on earth, good-will to men!"

Then pealed the bells more loud and deep:
"God is not dead, nor doth He sleep;
*   The Wrong shall fail,*
*   The Right prevail,*
With peace on earth, good-will to men.'"[59]

It was Longfellow who once said, "If we could read the secret history of our enemies, we would find in each person's life sorrow and suffering enough to disarm all hostility."

At Christmas we celebrate the outrage of light against the backdrop of darkness. *"In the beginning was the Word, and the Word was with God, and the Word was God. He was in the beginning with God. All things came into being through him, and without him not one thing came into being. What has come into being in him was life, and the life was the light of all people. The light shines in the darkness, and the darkness did not overcome it."*

Matthew Joseph Thaddeus Stepanek, known to his friends as "Mattie," knew what that darkness felt like. He was born with a rare form of muscular dystrophy and outlived his three siblings who died of the same disease. His mother also had an adult form of muscular dystrophy. But in the midst of that darkness, Mattie began writing poetry and short stories at the age of three. At fifteen years of age, he had written two best-selling books of poetry and had contracted to publish three forthcoming volumes.

Mattie was a gifted, courageous poet and human being who "refused to go quietly into that dark night." I wish to leave you with a prayer he wrote, called "Pinch of Peace":

> *Dear God,*
> *Tonight my prayers are for the world.*
> *We have to stop this fighting.*
> *We have to stop the wars.*
> *People need to lay down their weapons,*
> *And find peace in their hearts.*
> *People need to stop arguing and hating.*
> *People need to notice the good things.*
> *People need to remember You, God.*
> *Maybe You could come and*
> *Shoot a little bow-and-arrow pinch*
> *Into all the angry people's hearts, God.*
> *Then they would feel You again.*

And then they would realize what
They are doing and how horrible the
Killing and hating and fighting is,
And they might even begin to pray.
Then, they could reach in, and
Pull the little bow-and-arrow pinch
Out of their hearts and feel good
And be loving and living people again.
And then,
The world would be at peace, and
The children would be safe, and
The people would be happy, and
We could all say 'Thank You' together,
Amen."[61]

IT'S A WONDERFUL LIFE!

One thing I can count on every Christmas is that I will be moved to tears by a particular movie. There are a lot of emotional films around the holiday season. But for me, and I dare say for some of you, *It's A Wonderful Life* tops them all. Christmas wouldn't seem to be Christmas without it.

It's A Wonderful Life was the first film Frank Capra made after returning from service in the Second World War. He was committed to a vision:

> "My films will explore the heart not with logic, but with compassion. . . . I will deal with the little man's doubts, his curses, his loss of faith in himself, in his neighbor, in his God. And I will show the overcoming of doubts, the courageous renewal of faith . . . and that peace and salvation will become a reality only when [every man, woman and child] learns to love each other."[62]

It's A Wonderful Life is the story of an "ordinary man." George Bailey (played by Jimmy Stewart, a member of the Beverly Hills Presbyterian Church, I might add) is neither brilliant nor heroic nor rich nor famous. He is just an ordinary guy whose dreams of wealth, travel, and adventure continue to be squelched by family obligation and civic duty. When it come to a choice for self or others, George always chooses for others, reluctantly sometimes, but committed nonetheless.

Beneath his father's portrait is the motto, "All you can take with you is that which you've given away." When one of his Saving and Loan families purchases their first house, George and his wife, Mary, visit them and give them a loaf of Bread ("that your house may never know hunger"), Salt ("that life may always have flavor") and Wine ("that joy and prosperity may always reign forever").

Here is a common man facing the great events of history: the Great Depression, the Stock Market Crash, a bank run, World War II. While his brother is winning the Congressional Medal of Honor and his mother is having lunch with the president's wife, George is forced to stay at home and live an ordinary life in Bedford Falls. Like you and me, he finds himself torn between the obligations of life and the dream of being someone else, somewhere else—if only we could get out of town and start over.

George is a good guy, a caring husband and father, to whom life deals a series of bad hands. Finally, on Christmas Eve, the discouragement and depression of seeing the contrast between what is and what could be breaks him. He loses his grip on reality, his faith in God, his love for his family, his trust in people, in himself, and his faith in the essential goodness of life. His dreams turn into nightmares, his victory to defeat, and he attempts suicide . . . only to be rescued by his responsibility for others as he saves Clarence the wingless angel from drowning. In Camus's novel, *The Fall*, Jean-Baptiste hears the scream of despair on a bridge at midnight and walks away. George Bailey hears a scream of despair on a bridge at midnight and dives in to help.

The turning point for George comes when he returns to Bedford Falls as it would have been if he had never been born. He sees the pathetic doctor who would not have been stopped by a young George from prescribing poison to a boy. He sees the deterioration of the morals and quality of life which would have happened in Bedford Falls and the suffering and hopelessness of his friends and would-have-been bride. At that moment, he chooses to live.

In the final scenes of the movie, he runs through the streets of Bedford Falls, blessing them and praising them, shouting "Merry Christmas" to everyone—even Old Man Potter, who had tried to ruin him. He rejoices that there is a warrant for his arrest and kisses the knob on the banister that had always annoyed him. He holds his wife and children tight to him with tears of joy as the entire town files past their Christmas tree with their gifts of love and gratitude for what he has meant in their lives. His daughter Janie plays "Hark the Herald Angels Sing" on the piano, and everyone sings "Auld Lang Syne."

It's a beautiful story, isn't it? The problem is that for many people the first part is more true than the last. Life isn't all wonderful. It is hard and cruel and painful. It is full of disappointment and broken dreams. For many, it is a "veil of tears." Some of you have lost your job this year. Some of you have lost a loved one. Some of you have lost your best friend. Some of you have lost your health or your self-respect or your hope. Some of you have even lost your faith.

There is a paradox at Christmastime. While our exterior world seems caught up in bright lights, music, laughter, and parties, our interior world is often silently suffering. The heightened contrast between the joy, hope, and love of the season and our personal depression, hopelessness, and anxiety is often too much to bear. Our needs for love and significance cry out so loudly we cannot hear the sounds of "Silent Night."

Life has a cruel way of stripping us down to emotional and spiritual nakedness at Christmastime. We do not really know life until we have suffered its pain and loss and tragedy, until we have messed up our own lives, or circumstances beyond our control have robbed us of them. It is then that we get in touch with that dark, fallen, broken side of ourselves. We experience our common humanity more intensely than our brokenness.

And yet, the paradox is that it is precisely at that point when God seems absent that we can begin to know God's presence. The absence of God is the beginning of prayer.

The Gospel, the Good News of Christmas, is that we can see life anew and afresh through the eyes and heart of the Babe of Bethlehem. Born into our humanity, our poverty, our pain, he brings to birth our divinity. "For you know the grace of our Lord Jesus Christ, that though he was rich, yet for your sake he became poor, so that by his poverty you might become rich."[63] He became like us that we might become like him.

Perhaps we are attracted to George Bailey because we see in him hope for ourselves. If he can turn discouragement into hope and hell into heaven, then so can we. I commend to you a motto which has helped me get through times of great darkness in my own life: "In tempestate floreso" or "in time of storm I flourish."

Frank Capra said of his movie, "I wanted *It's A Wonderful Life* to reflect the compelling words of Fra Giovanni of nearly five centuries ago: "The gloom of the world is but a shadow. Behind it, yet within reach, is joy. There is a radiance and glory in the darkness, could we but see; and to see we have only to look. I beseech you to look!"[64]

That is what we celebrate on Christmas morning. "The Word became flesh and dwelt among us full of grace and truth."[65] God's answer to our suffering is to join it, feel it, hurt with it, hold us through it, and redeem it. There is no pit so deep that God is not deeper still.

Love was born that day in the poverty and powerlessness of a manger. By identifying ourselves with the Incarnate God, by absorbing ourselves in his presence and his teaching, by living out the drama of our lives with him, especially his passion, we can be reborn into a new world, just like George Bailey. The miracle of George Bailey's story is that nothing changed! The streets of Bedford Falls were still the same old streets. His business would remain the same old grind. His circumstances recycled the same old problems. His family life held the same old routine. What changed was George Bailey! From within. He saw his life differently at Christmas. He realized what the world would have been like had he never been born. That's the way God works to change the world.

I wonder if you lined up all the people whose lives you have touched over the years, from classmates to waitresses to co-workers to church members to friends and family, what would they say about how their life was different because they had met you? I have a hunch that you would be amazed at the difference your life has made in hundreds of lives over the years.

Sure, life is hard. Life will always have its pain as well as its pleasure, its suffering as well as its glory. But, for those who listen for the angel's voices, who allow themselves to be embraced by the One in swaddling clothes, blanketed in the eternal life of divine love, and who live to give themselves to others, it can be a won-der-filled life.

In the final scene of the movie, Harry Bailey lifts his glass of wine to his brother who had lost everything, and says, "A toast . . . to my big brother, George: The richest man in town."

George glances down and reads Clarence's inscription, "No man who has friends is a failure."

So it can be for you. My prayer is that you will discover the won-der. In anticipation, I make a toast to you, my friends: Some of the truly richest folks in the world!

CHAPTER 18

THE AMAZING POWER OF YES

"The angel answered,
'The Holy Spirit will come upon you, and the power
of the Most High will overshadow you.
So the holy one to be born will be called the Son of God.
. . . For nothing is impossible with God."
—LUKE 1:35, 37

A tourist came to close to the edge of the Grand Canyon, lost his footing, and plunged over the side, clawing and scratching to save himself. After he went out of sight, and just before he fell into space, he encountered a scrubby bush which he desperately grabbed with both hands.

Filled with terror, he called out toward heaven, "Is there anyone up there?" A calm, powerful voice came out of the sky. "Yes, there is." The tourist pleaded, "Can you help me? Can you help me?" The calm voice replied, "Yes, I probably can. What is your problem?" "I fell over the cliff and am dangling in space holding to a bush that is about to let go. Please help me."

The voice from above said, "I'll try. Do you believe?" "Yes, yes, I believe!" "Do you have faith?" "Yes, yes. I have strong faith." The calm voice said, "Well, in that case, simply let loose of the bush and everything will turn out fine." There was a tense pause, then the tourist yelled, "Is there anyone else up there?"

Too many of us grew up with the old adage, "Look before you leap." The problem with that approach to life is that you can look 'til kingdom comes, but it won't come until you leap.

There is no more powerful word in the English language than the word, "YES." "YES" is the single word that unlocks the future. "YES" is the bulldozer that burrows through the obstacles of our intransigence. "YES" is the ultimate human response to the Divine "YES" to us in Jesus Christ.

There is always ample evidence to show why an idea will not work. There are always plenty of reasons to wait until you have more information. There are always reasons to see the glass as half empty. But pessimists do not create life; they destroy it before conception.

God never meant for us to continually confirm our congenital preference for safe investments and limited liabilities. Where there is no risk, there is no opportunity. I believe the only thing that can save our planet is a divine optimism and a passion for the possible. I want to be around "glass half full" people: People who see the possibilities in every gray cloud. People who see every "no" as a way to accomplish a "yes." People who will set aside their skepticism and seize the moment to usher in the impossible.

Nowhere in the Bible can you find a greater example of this act of faith than in the affirmative response of Mary to the claim of God on her young life. Mary, or "Miriam from Nazareth" as she was called, still in her adolescence, is not looking to get pregnant, nor to have a baby for which she has not prayed. Her family denounces it, her unmarried status forbids it, her economic condition rejects it, her religion ostracizes it, and her own inner spirit cries out, "GOD. . . WHY ME? . . . WHY THIS? . . . WHY NOW?"

Yet as Matthew and Luke retell this ancient tale of primitive Christianity, Mary is invited to lend her life, her body, her reputation, her career, and her future, to a mission that is biologically and theologically inconceivable. Nonetheless, with all the obstacles which she will need to overcome for the rest of her life, Mary says "YES" to God . . . "YES" to Life . . . and risks her personal future for the good of a better world.

Of course, we know very little about Mary and her son Jesus before his public ministry. In the opinion of most mainstream scholars, the stories of Jesus's birth and childhood are more theological impressions than historical facts. Only the Gospels of Matthew and Luke refer to them, and they were written at least sixty years after Jesus's death. Paul, the earliest New Testament author, never mentions Jesus being born in a special way. Nor does Mark, the earliest Gospel, nor John, the latest.

No one really knows what actually happened in the mind and heart and body of Mary in this story of "YES," nor how the story developed over the years. What we do know, though, is that Jesus was such an extraordinary person that these kinds of stories grew up around him and were passed on from generation to generation. While we will never know all the *facts* of his birth, we do know the *truth* of his life. Matthew and Luke both affirm that Jesus was not simply born "of the flesh," but also "of God"—that is, "of the Spirit."

Mysteries capture our imaginations not because they are logical and believable, but precisely because they are illogical and inconceivable. As Charles Dickens put it, "In [this] season of immortal hope, and on the birthday of immortal mercy, we will shut out nothing."

In the collection, *Women's Uncommon Prayers*, June Schulte imagines the Mary in all of us:

"Out of the depth and quiet
of this chill, stark night,
a gnawing ache, a yearning
deepens, rising
like a threatening wave.

The young woman trembles.
Every inmost part of her is
shaken, all comfort broken.
Her hand gropes for something firm to grasp,
but all that was certain has become
obscure, all encompassing,
racked with pain.
Scarcely able to catch her breath,
she feels each wave larger, more
frightening than the last.
And as the great wave breaks over her,
she is broken,
momentarily forgetting what she accepted,
what love she bears,
yet choosing to believe when all seems lost.

Suddenly and completely
she, still bathed in sweat,
enfolds love in her arms,
knows joy as one victorious,
sees clearly as one who has been
stretched and changed,

that peace is always
born of travail."[66]

Only by saying "YES" to God and Life are we empowered to turn death into life for others.

The timeless message of this "Grand Possibility of New Birth," as the thirteenth-century German mystic and heretic, Meister Eckhart, put it, is that

"We are all meant to be mothers of God.
For God is always needing to be born."[67]

This is the true meaning of Christmas. Nobody in those days knew what God looked like until Jesus showed up. And nobody will know what God looks like now until you and I show up. "Christ in you, the hope of glory," as St. Paul puts it.[68]

I want you to remember that at the center of the universe is a Heartbeat of Love—invisible and incredible. Our task is to get close enough to that heartbeat so that it beats *through* us and becomes visible and credible *in* us.

Let's look again at Bishop John Spong's exhortation on the fullest meaning of love. "Love is manifested in the human willingness to venture beyond the boundaries of safety, to risk losing ourselves, and even in the desire to explore the crevices of the unknown. Love creates stability, but not stagnation. Love calls us into being; it expands our lives as it flows through us. If love is ever blocked, it dies. Love has to be shared, or it ceases to be love. Love binds us into larger and larger communities. Love frees us from the pejorative definitions that result in exclusion. Love transcends barriers, unites and calls. Love enhances life. . . .

"Love has no chosen people, for that implies that some are unchosen. Love bears no malice, seeks no revenge, guards no doorway.

"A life defined by love will not seek to *protect itself* or to *justify itself.* It will be content simply to *be itself* and to give itself away with abandon. If denied, love embraces the denier. If betrayed, love embraces the betrayer. If forsaken, love embraces the forsaker. If tortured, love embraces the torturer. If crucified, love embraces the killers. Love never judges. Love simply announces that neither the person you are, nor the deeds you have done, have created a barrier which the power of this *invincible presence* cannot overcome."[69]

In our age of national imperialism and global terrorism, "Peace on Earth, Goodwill to All" will not come to pass through a quasi-guaranteed security backed up by weaponry, political treaties, or lucrative business investments. Before it is to come to pass, peace must first be accepted by us, and conceived in us. Peace must first be dared. Peace must be birthed. We must say "YES" to peace.

To quote Einstein, "Imagination is more important than knowledge." It is not enough to analyze the world as it is and ask, "Why?" We need also to imagine the world as it might be and ask, "Why not?"

We need to imagine a world whose peoples consider themselves to be citizens of the world first, and only then, citizens of their particular country. We need to imagine a world which refuses to believe that "might makes right" and which makes the conquest of war, the preservation of nature, and the pursuit of social justice "our grand preoccupation and magnificent obsession." (Norman Cousins)

"Above all, and at almost any risk, we must get the world beyond war. It is not enough to wish for peace, we have to will it, to pray, think, struggle for peace as if the whole world depended upon it, as indeed it does."[70]

Archbishop Oscar Romero, whose life and work with the Salvadoran poor was cut short by an assassin's bullet on March 24, 1980, claimed that each of us are "Prophets of a Future Not Our Own":

> *"It helps, now and then, to step back*
> *and take the long view.*
> *The kingdom is not only beyond our efforts,*
> *it is beyond our vision.*

We accomplish in our lifetime only a tiny fraction of
the magnificent enterprise that is God's work.
Nothing we do is complete,
which is another way of saying
that the kingdom always lies beyond us.

No statement says all that could be said.
No prayer fully expresses our faith.
No confession brings perfection.
No pastoral visit bring wholeness.
No program accomplishes the church's mission.
No set of goals and objectives includes everything.

This is what we are about:
We plant seeds that one day will grow.
We water seeds already planted, knowing that they
     hold future promise.
We lay foundations that will need further development.
We provide yeast that produces effects beyond our capabilities.

We cannot do everything
and there is a sense of liberation in realizing that.
This enables us to do something,
and to do it very well.
It may be incomplete, but it is a beginning,
     a step along the way,
an opportunity for God's grace to enter and do the rest.

We may never see the end results,
but that is the difference between the master builder
     and the worker.
We are workers, not master builders,
Ministers, not messiahs.
We are prophets of a future not our own."

What if Mary had "just said NO"? What if God had continued to ask to be born in someone else—and finally asked it of you? How would *you* respond? How will *we* respond?

Advent is the season of the Christian church when one prepares for the coming birth of Jesus. You and I can join that scared, little fifteen-year-old Mary in becoming with her "the mothers of Christ." We can give birth to him again and again through our doubts, our decisions, and our dedication. If love and peace and justice are to be born on the earth in our time, it is up to us to carry that new life to full-term. As Helen Keller showed us in her own miraculous life, "The world is full of suffering. And it is also full of overcoming it."

These are days of awe and wonder, of hope and promise. There is nothing to fear but fear itself. Let us join with Dag Hammarskjold, that strong Christian and former Secretary General of the United Nations, and say in response to the whispers of angels on Christmas Day, "For all that has been, THANKS! and for all that shall be, YES!"

CHAPTER 19

THE TWELVE DAYS
OF CHRISTMAS

As many of you know, I love Christmas and all of its decoration. I suffer mid-winter deprivation every January when Bev finally insists that we throw out the old, sagging tree. I always object, but she always wins out.

Not everyone feels the same as I do about Christmas. I heard recently of one minister who asked his congregation how many of them were going to take down their Christmas tree on Epiphany (the end of the Twelve Days of Christmas). One woman proudly reported that she had removed all her decorations by 2 p.m. on Christmas Day! When asked why, she replied, "After we opened all the presents, I got depressed. I was so tired of Christmas stuff; I just couldn't stand it. Christmas is never as good as the advertisements lead you to believe."

While I disagree with her timetable, there are times when I agree with her criticism. Someone once said, "Christmas falls like a seed on soil exhausted by too many harvests."

Here we are, exhausted, after the glorious celebration of all the angels of heaven and all the creatures of earth singing, "Gloria in excelsis Deo." "Veiled in flesh the Godhead see; Hail the incarnate Deity. . . ." "Joyful all ye nations, rise, Join the triumph of the skies; With the angelic host proclaim, 'Christ is born in Bethlehem!'"

But where has all the Glory gone? Most of it has been returned for credit. No more shepherds watching their flocks by night. Now it's "Attention K-Mart Shoppers," and on to the New Year Sales Events.

That's why we need the Twelve Days of Christmas—to remind us that Christmas has not ended; it has just begun. The Feast of the Epiphany is celebrated on January 6, the twelfth night after Christmas, to commemorate (in the West) the visit of the wise men to Jesus, and (in the East) the baptism of Christ. The name comes from the Greek "epiphaneia" or "manifestation." That is, the manifestation of the glory of God to those who were not Jews. Jesus's initial reception, you will remember, was to his own people, Israel, not to outsiders. It was not until months, or even years later, that the gentiles were the least bit interested.

And yet, had we never shown any interest in the source of that brilliant light above a common house in the Mid-East, we would never have to worry about all the excessive trappings of Christmas. Epiphany can be an antidote for our Christmas malaise. Rather than hurrying to get rid of the tree and the cards and the feelings of love and warmth and mystery, we can choose to "live into Christmas" day after day—not just for twelve days, but for the next twelve months of every year.

Maybe Christmas is not so much like a seed, "exhausted by too many harvests," as it is a flower, an expression of faith rather than a basis of faith. "This flower is as true and beautiful as it is mysterious. Think of the truths that Matthew manages to express in the first eleven short verses of Chapter 2:

- the truth that people come from afar and by many ways to worship Christ;
- the truth that no place in this world is too lowly to kneel in;
- the truth that as knowledge grows, so also must reverence and love, lest too much learning dry the heart;
- the truth that wise men and women think as people of action and act as people of thought.

"And the star over Bethlehem—what does God's sign set high in the night sky symbolize, if not the deepest longing of every thinking person, which is for a Savior from beyond a world too sin-sick to heal itself? Yet a sign is just that, only a sign, and the choice remains ours to journey toward it or to stay stuck wherever we are."[71]

And so, the light above and within the windows of God's house this Epiphany beckons us to join those wise travelers of old in kneeling in adoration at Christ's humble manger. We come once more to offer the Christ child our gifts of GOLD, representing the best of our solid accomplishments, of INCENSE, representing the rest that must happen in our lives and our world, which we can only ask God to do through prayer, and the MYRRH, representing the suffering to which we submit in order for God to use us to bring about peace on the earth.

So, this Epiphany, let us celebrate the Light of our New Year. . .

> *"Ring out wild bells to the wild sky,*
> *   The flying cloud, the frosty light:*
> *   The year is dying in the night;*
> *Ring out, wild bells, and let him die.*
>
> *Ring out the old, ring in the new,*
> *   Ring, happy bells, across the snow:*
> *   The year is going, let him go;*
> *Ring out the false, ring in the true.*
>
> *. . .*
>
> *Ring out old shapes of foul disease,*
> *   Ring out the narrowing lust of gold:*
> *   Ring out the thousand wars of old,*
> *Ring in the thousand years of peace.*
>
> *Ring in the valiant man and free,*
> *   The larger heart, the kindlier hand;*
> *   Ring out the darkness of the land,*
> *Ring in the Christ that is to be."*[72]

CHAPTER 20

THE GREAT GIVE-AWAY: A CHRISTMAS STORY FOR ADULTS

There is a lovely tradition among the Northern Plains tribes of American Indians. Like our Celtic ancestors, their belief is that all of creation (humanity, animals, birds, insects, and plants) are part of a sacred hoop. The Lakota expression for this is "mitakuye oyasin," literally, "all my relations."

Not just at Christmas, but at tribal memorials, in times of honor, and at Christenings, or the giving of names, they practice what they call the Give-Away. Through the Give-Away the community is saying, "This thing of honor we do is more important than anything we might possess." Families may work for years creating things to be given at a Give-Away. The ultimate Give-Away is the giving of oneself—literally, the offering of oneself, for the sake of the people. It may be in battle or in the sun dance. It may be in the sacred vow. It may be in a life of service. The Give-Away then becomes a way of life.

In the song of Mary we see personified in one young woman the promise of the "Great Give-Away" of God, in which the lowly are exalted, the proud are brought down, the hungry are filled with good things, while the rich are sent away empty. It is for us the culmination of the prophet's dreams, the seer's visions, and the people's hopes. I invite you to relax for the next few minutes and enter into the Christmas Story in a new way. The fable is entitled, "The Give-Away" by Ray Buckley:

"There was a grove of trees where the forest grew thick. The trees had stood there for as long as anyone could remember, their roots intertwined so that nothing could affect one without affecting them all.

"[These ancient trees] were known to the inhabitants of the forest, the Four-Leggeds and Those Who Fly, as the Old Ones. In the middle of the Old Ones stood the oldest of them all, taller and broader than the others. If one stood beneath it, one could not see where its crown touched Father Sky, and smaller trees grew around its roots in the safety of its vastness. It was called the Ancient One, for it had known the Creator longest of all.

"It was to this grove that the creatures of the forest and the plains, the Four-Leggeds and Those Who Fly, gathered for council. Each had sent one speaker, the oldest and the wisest of its kind. Snow fell thick on familiar paths, and each arrived in silence, waiting with the patience of those who have seen much. When the circle was complete, they stood listening to their hearts.

"'They have lost their way,' Whooping Crane said, 'There is no pattern to their journey.' Snow Goose nodded in agreement.

"'They have lost their purpose,' Deer Mouse said softly, 'They do not gather seeds. They do not know who they are.'

"Tatanka, the Bull Buffalo, dropped his head low. 'They take more than they need and give nothing back. They do not give away.'

"'They do not see long-distance,' Eagle began. 'They keep more than they can eat, while some are hungry. They no longer know that they are connected.'

"'They do not know that they are beautiful,' Fox said sadly, her white coat blending with the snow. 'They decorate themselves with stones and hide their Spirits.'

"'They think that power is what they can hold on to,' Old Beaver pondered. 'They say, "This is mine," and build lodges too large so that they, themselves, will appear big.'

"'They must make others small, so that they will look big,' Bear's deep voice answered. 'In the end, they must destroy themselves or others. They have lost their names, and do not know who they are.'

"Grandmother Turtle, who was the last to arrive, made her way slowly to the center of the council. She lifted her head so she could see all who gathered beneath the Old Ones. Her voice was barely audible. 'We must give-away ourselves to them. We must speak to them in soft voices. We must remind them of who they are.'

"She paused, lowering her head into her shell. Then suddenly, she lifted her head as high as her neck would allow. 'I will give them my shell,' she said with certainty. 'I will come with no protection, and they can use my shell to adorn themselves.'

"Around the circle, council was silent. The Wind did not blow through the trees. Not a single branch on the Old Ones fluttered. The forest was still as Grandmother Turtle began her walk back to the empty spot in the circle.

"'I will teach them the patterns of life,' Whooping Crane said slowly. 'Snow Goose and I will remind them of the seasons.'

"'I will teach them to gather seeds so that no one need be hungry,' Deer Mouse began. 'I will give them what I have stored.'

"Eagle searched the night sky and, without lowering her head, said, 'I will give them my feathers. Perhaps if I cannot fly, they will not feel small.'

"Tatanka, the Bull Buffalo, stood with his legs squarely on the Earth. 'I will give them my flesh to sustain them, and my skin to warm them. I will give myself away.'

"Each council member in turn rose to speak of the gift, that most costly portion of themselves, that each would give away. When the circle was complete, a new voice was heard.

"In the shadow of the Ancient One stood the Creator.

"'Ho, children!' the Creator began softly. 'You will give yourselves away, but they will not know that. They will say, "See what I have taken!" and think that they have made themselves larger.'

"For a moment, the Creator paused. 'It is I who must give myself away. I must give-away my protection and come vulnerable to their lodges. I must choose to become small, so that they can choose to know me large. I must give away my Name, so that they can know their names.'

"The Ancient One had stood silent. The sound of his voice had not been heard in many winters. 'Creator, how can this be? How can the Great Mystery become small?'

"The Creator stood beneath the Ancient One. The shadow of the great tree became light, the grove of the Old Ones became full of the presence of the Creator. 'A baby will be born. He will be the Son of the Great Mystery. He will be born not where the Two-Leggeds are gathered, but among the Four-Leggeds and Those Who Fly. He will bring light into confusion. He will bring hope into despair. He will bring love, and his name will be great.'

"The Ancient One began to tremble, and Those Who Fly left its old branches. The grove of the Old Ones moved in its quake. 'Creator, what can I, whose name speaks only of my age, give-away to the Great Mystery become baby? What can I do from my grove in the forest?'

"The Creator turned to the Ancient One. The voice of the Creator was low. 'You will be his support. You will be his place of rest. You will hold his body. You will hold him up. In the beginning . . . and at the end.'

"And the Ancient One wept, partly for joy, and partly for sorrow."[73]

> *"For God so loved the world that God gave-away His only begotten Son. . . . Herein is Love, not that we loved God, but that God loved us. . . . Beloved, let us love one another, because love is from God; everyone who loves is born of God and knows God . . . for God is love."*[74]

CHAPTER 21

ANGELS OF LIGHT

Have you noticed the number of books written about angels? James Patterson and Peter de Jonge's book, *Miracle on the 17th Green* is about a middle-aged advertising executive who is getting fired, whose marriage is collapsing, and whose children are alienated, who, while playing golf on Christmas morning, has a Zen-like moment, when he "sees the line" and finally learns how to putt! In fact, his entire game improves to the point where he is on the P.G.A. Senior Tour, hanging out with Lee Trevino and winning enough money to buy his wife a $135,000 diamond ring from Harry Winston. Right! And I have a devil of a time scoring below 120 on a good day. And that's on the front 9!

If anyone should know about angels, it is a preacher from Los Angeles, where angels are referred to every time the name of the city is mentioned! For a time, the historic Immanuel Presbyterian Church on Wilshire Boulevard, where I served as senior pastor, was known as the "Cathedral of the Angels." World-renowned artist, Tony Duquette, had created a fantastic set of pieces entitled "Our Lady Queen of the Angels," for the Bicentennial Celebration of the city. It took him two years working with teams of dedicated volunteers from every ethnic and economic background to create a gallery of giant twenty-eight-foot-tall metal Arch Angels surrounded by monumental jewel-studded fabric mosaic tapestries. Every culture was represented in the smiling face of the Madonna who stood in a winged pavilion under a winged halo. The Angels represented each of the four seasons and the four elements—air, earth, fire, and water.

After the 1984 Olympic Games, the exhibit was relocated into our spacious sanctuary. The angels surrounded the worshippers on Sunday morning (not unlike Isaiah's vision, or St. Paul's comment that "we are surrounded by so great a cloud of witnesses"). Throughout the week, hundreds of visitors from all over the world, would pay a small fee to view the angels and listen to a taped presentation of ethereal music and a poetic invocation written by Ray Bradbury and narrated by Charlton Heston (the voice of God!).

It was a wonderful experience of being surrounded by angels and feeling the mystery of life with all of one's senses. But, unfortunately, there were a number of church members who refused to come to church until "they [got] rid of those blankety-blank angels." So, tradition won out, and they were removed and sent to San Francisco. There the exhibition caught fire and melted to the ground. A terrible thing!

Four hundred years ago, English and Scottish Protestant reformers were fervent in their desire to cleanse churches newly under their control of what they believed to be pagan and popish influences. They whitewashed wall paintings, discontinued prayers for the dead, and stripped altars of their finery. Their reforming zeal was focused on anything that suggested idolatry, particularly the saints or the Virgin Mary. Carvings were burned or smashed, and few of the thousands of stained-glass windows remained intact. Not so with images of angels. Because some of the reformers held a certain affection for angels, that which could easily have been obliterated was not, and today there remains a great deal of early and late medieval art depicting angels as Divine Messengers.

In the Hebrew Scripture we get a glimpse into the dark, exilic world of captive Israel. The metaphors used by Isaiah are decidedly "political." The angelic messenger is addressing those who are captives, prisoners, those languishing in "devastations" and "ruined cities." As William Willimon says, "It is a word for Bosnia and Rawandan refugees before it is a word for the affluent who may be temporarily depressed."[75]

A modern day captive, Dr. Ma Thida, a 29-year-old Burmese surgeon, is confined alone in a Rangoon cell, forbidden even any reading material. She was sentenced to twenty years in prison in 1993 for "endangering public tranquility, having contact with unlawful organizations, and distributing unlawful literature." More succinctly, it means that she supported democracy in Burma. She is a symbol of the cruelty of Burma's rulers. "Physicians for Human Rights" and other groups have brought her name to light. She was among the winners of the Reebok Human Rights Awards for "courage in the face of tyranny." But she is still alone in that Rangoon cell.[76]

Angels come in many different forms. Not only are there angels of light, but there are dark angels of death that reside in each of us, and in our institutions: families, political parties, governments, even churches. It should not be amazing, but it is, how some of those dark angels come out when our lifestyle or property is threatened. Neighbor turns against neighbor, friend against friend. Hundreds of years ago, Saint Gertrude said of these things: "Property: the more common it is, the holier it is." Likewise, I would add, when we own it, we are willing to sacrifice everything for it, including our decency and civility, as many of you know who have lost a parent and gone through the family strife of dividing up the inheritance.

Yet the same folks who fought each other yesterday gather together today in their houses of worship to kneel before a God whose angelic messenger's promise will "bring good tidings to the afflicted . . . bind up the broken-hearted . . . proclaim liberty to the captives . . . opening of the prison to those who are bound . . . build up the ancient ruins . . . [and] cause righteousness and praise to spring forth before all nations."[77]

It is in the lobby of that apartment house in Brooklyn on a Saturday night where that three-day-old baby girl was found alive in a paper bag. In a note with the baby, the mother expressed remorse over abandoning her daughter and said that she was unable to support her. She called her daughter Sarah (the Biblical mother of the people of God). She said in her note that she took vacation time from work to give birth, and hoped that the infant would be loved by adoptive parents.

Thank God that little Sarah is healthy and doing fine. No one knows who or where her mother is, but now thousands of us know her plight. Sarah is the lucky one. Not so for hundreds and thousands of other babies born into poverty in this, the wealthiest country on earth. A baby in a bag is a blight on our national soul.

But the angel of light speaks to us today through the prophets, "prepare the way of the Lord—make His paths straight." Christians like ourselves need to challenge the rest of the nation, not try to resemble the rest of the nation. Why should a nation resent the free medical care that allows all mothers and their children, regardless of how poor they are, to see doctors more often? In the long run, it is cheaper to eradicate poverty than maintain it.

Why does any working woman in this country have to choose between keeping herself alive and keeping her three-day-old baby alive—that life within her whom she loved, protected, and nurtured for nine months and three days? When are we going to "just say no" to that kind of selfish death-dealing angel of poverty (and undoubtedly of class and race), and "just say yes" to the angel of light who comes to us again and again in the form of a young, imprisoned Burmese surgeon, and of a three-day-old Sarah in a paper bag, and of a cold, helpless baby born to poor, young, unmarried parents, in a cold cave behind a tourist hotel in a big and lonely city in the Middle East? Our hope lies in the future of our children. Ending poverty would not only save us money; it might even save our souls.

There is no doubt about it. There were angels there that day—in that dank prison cell, in that little paper bag, in that smelly back alley of a manger. Whenever a child was born in ancient Palestine, it was customary for local musicians to gather at the child's house to sing God's praises. But when Jesus was born, no Bethlehem musicians heard the news, so heavenly musicians had to take over. The first acclamation came from the sky itself—a host of angels singing "Gloria in excelsis Deo," "Glory to God in the highest, and on earth peace among those with whom God is pleased."

In her book of Christmas poems, *Kneeling in Bethlehem*, Ann Weems asks the question:

> "Wouldn't it be grand to be an angel
> and have as your address
> 'The Realms of the Glory of God'?

And swing on rainbows,
*   and gather stars in your pockets,*
*   winging in and out of earth*
*   in a flurry of moondust*
*   with the messages of God?*
Comforting the distressed, warning the righteous,
*   delivering the just, guarding little children?*

*Of course, we **can** comfort and warn*
*   and deliver and guard.*
*Maybe, if we get **that** right,*
*   we can swing on rainbows later."*[78]

CHAPTER 22

SANTA IS MY SON

It was Christmas time. Mom and Dad assured their chronically ill toddler that she would get to meet Santa. For weeks the little girl spoke of nothing else. Mom prayed for a Santa who would live up to her daughter's expectations. Finally, on one of the little girl's better days, Mom decided that this was the day. In order to avoid lengthy lines, they arrived just as the mall was opening and Santa was settling into his big chair.

When the little girl saw him, she squealed, "Santa Claus!" and darted past a few assistant elves toward Santa. The slightly startled Santa greeted her with a big smile and swept her into his ample lap. She snuggled in and stroked his beard, and uttered in joyful awe, "Santa!" For several minutes, Santa and the little girl talked and laughed like two old friends, oblivious to the small crowd gathering to share in the magic of the moment.

The toddler's mother stood nearby, her eyes filled with tears of joy. Just then, a man edged over to her and to her surprise, she noticed that his eyes were as moist as hers. "Is that your little girl?" he asked quietly. The woman nodded.

With a catch in his voice and a quiet pride, the man said, "Santa is my son."[79]

There, in the wilderness of vacant aisles in a department store, one could see the Advent expectations of humanity. There was a caring parent who hoped that her failing daughter would not be disappointed yet again. There was a little girl who cared more about a new friendship that she did about a new teddy bear. There were observing bystanders who never quite got it. There was a man playing Santa who stepped out of his role of bearing gifts to bear hope. And there was a father who was moved to tears by his own son's selfless serving.

The Biblical story of Advent pictures a different scene ages ago on the riverbanks of a Judean countryside. Hardly a rotund Santa figure in a red suit with at jolly wink, John the Baptist is a lean man without much clothing, scavenging the ground for food, and crying out in the wilderness as a witness to one who is to follow. "He himself was not the light, but he came to testify to the light," to witness to the light, to point to the light.

For John, life's biggest question was not, "Who am I?" It was "Whose am I?" It was not, "How do I get people to follow me?" It was, "Who do I point others toward?" It wasn't, "Follow me." It was, "Find The Way for yourselves and follow it with me."

John envisioned his mission and his message not as a "hitching post" to which others should tie their faith, but rather as a "sign post" pointing to something, someone, beyond himself.

There is a wonderful metaphor for this in the Buddhist tradition. Buddhists often speak of the teachings of the Buddha as "a finger pointing to the moon." "The metaphor helps guard against the mistake of thinking that being a Buddhist means believing in Buddhist teaching—that is, believing in the finger." Rather, "one is to see (and pay attention to) that to which the finger points."

As Marcus Borg points out, "We Christians sometimes make the mistake of thinking that being Christian is about believing in the finger, rather than seeing the Christian life as a relationship to that to which the finger points."[80]

For John the Baptist, the story of the Jewish people's struggle was a kind of lens through which they and he saw God and the world. For Christians, the story of the Bible, and especially the story of Jesus, is a kind of lens through which we see God and the world. We are who we are, to a large extent, because we choose to see life and faith through this particular lens. But the danger is that we come to believe in the lens, rather than using the lens as a way of seeing what is beyond the lens.

To believe in Jesus is really about experiencing personally the love and presence of God which we see in Jesus. For Christians, Jesus is the Way. There is no other.

As Bishop John Spong says, "If God is . . . the source of life and the source of love, then God surely cannot be contained in any religious system, nor can any people continue to live as if God were the tribal deity of their particular nation or group. Being, life, and love transcend all boundaries. No sacred scripture of any religious tradition can any longer claim that in its pages the fullness of God has been captured."[81]

In times of fear and anxiety, people gravitate to simple solutions for complex problems. But "thinking Christians" live with ambiguity. Many Christians prefer certainty to truth. Yet the Christ whom we kneel before this Advent promises us risk, not certainty and adventure, not boredom. We do what we can with our words and our lives to point others to the truth which we have experienced in Jesus, but we do so with humility, reverence, and awe for the very existence of the other person with whom we seek to share our "lens" on the faith.

Ours is an expansive, not a restrictive, faith and vision for the world. Christ is the light of the world. "God so loved the world that God gave us God's only begotten Son."[82] Jesus accepted every person, whether or not they accepted him. That is why we are not fearful of "the other." We welcome all people of goodwill. We believe that sincere differences beautify the pattern of life, and that the whole human sound goes up to God only from the full orchestra of humanity.

There is no question in my mind or heart that Jesus is my doorway into God. He reflects God and points to God more convincingly than any other person I know, as the moon reflects the sun. My faith and life are shaped by his story. I could not imagine personally entering the realm of God's life through any other door. Yet, once I have entered that doorway, I discover that there is an infinite realm of divine and human experience awaiting me, beyond my wildest imagination. Rather than being locked into the past by doctrinal formulas of another time and place, I am free to hope and believe into the future for a new day of faith on the earth.

My hope is that my sisters and brothers who find Judaism, Islam, Hinduism, Buddhism, or whatever way, to be their point of entry, will also explore their pathway into God in a similar manner. As each of us explores the essence of our own spiritual tradition, the intimacy of our life with the Eternal, and the just human society our religion calls us to create, we will transcend the boundaries of our traditions, and we will gladly share our faith with each other and the world.

Sometimes I think I can remember what it felt like to climb up on the lap of that department store Santa. Sometimes I think I can feel the trust, the love, and the safety of being held and understood by a gentle man in a red suit with a white beard, who would point the way for me toward Christmas. I know now that he was just an ordinary human being, like myself, filled with doubts and questions about it all, and probably less than comfortable in his role of way-shower and gift-giver. But, in spite of it all, he pointed the way for me, like a finger pointing to the moon. I'm sure my mother cried for me. And I'm sure his father cried for him. But they were tears of joy in the wasteland of that empty department store.

Now, thankfully, I can point my own finger to the moon. And rejoice with those who see it in a different light.

EPILOGUE

Two and a half years ago, in the most productive phase of my life, I began noticing that my breathing was labored during speeches and sermons. My pulmonary doctor ran several tests and assured me that all of them showed my lung capacity to be strong at about 90 percent. Then I began to have panic attacks while breathing and public speaking. After seeing several specialists, I was referred to Dr. Hiroshi Mitsumoto, Director of the Eleanor and Lou Gehrig MDA/ALS Center at Columbia University in New York. Tests there confirmed that I had ALS (amyotrophic lateral sclerosis, or Lou Gehrig's Disease).

Patients with ALS typically live only two to five years after diagnosis. Today, unbelievable as it is, 140 years after this fatal disease was discovered, there is still no known cause nor cure for it. I find that unacceptable.

But this is not the end of the story . . . this is the beginning of the cure. As Bertrand Russell wrote in his *Unpopular Essays,* *"Extreme hopes are born of extreme misery."*

I have a strong sense of *"passion for the possible."* As the great healer, Helen Keller, put it, "The world is full of suffering. It is also full of overcoming it."

I have lost most of my voice and must use a voice synthesizer. My breathing is quite difficult, so I rely on a servo-ventilator breathing machine. I have lost substantial muscle control in my legs and my upper body, so I am blessed to be able to have mobility in my "Power Chair." I can no longer eat or drink, but I take nutrients through a feeding tube and limit my research and writing to two-to-three hours a day, typing into the computer with the eraser end of a pencil!

But, the GOOD NEWS is that I am STILL ALIVE! As my new friend, Dr. Alan Russell (Director of the McGowan Institute at the

University of Pittsburg), tells me: *"Never give up hope. There is so much new research being done around the world that a breakthrough can always be just around the corner."*

I believe the cure for ALS will be found in Stem Cell Treatment. It took Harvard's Kevin Eggan less than twenty-seven months to create new patient- and disease-specific stem cell lines. These are the days of Miracle and Wonder.

President Barack Obama's first act was to lift an eight-year ban limiting federal funding of stem cell research, as part of a broader move to focus on science instead of politics. Because of this action, millions of lives will be saved from devastating diseases and injuries—not just ALS—but from Alzheimer's (of which my mother died), Parkinson's, diabetes, paralysis, and so many more.

"Never give up Hope!" I believe that while death is a part of life, *PREMATURE DEATH IS NEVER ACCEPTABLE WHEN THERE IS AN ALTERNATIVE FOR LIFE.*

As a Christian "Pan-en-theist," I believe that God creates all life and wants life to continue . . . if not in one form, then in another. We come from God, and we return to God. At death, life is changed, not taken away. All life is within God and God is within all life—interwoven into the very fiber of our being. Each of our lives is defined by and interwoven into one another's lives.

Our role as scientists, researchers, theologians, and religious leaders is to help people make the connections between one form of life and another. Because life is all about connections.

God is not just "out there" somewhere; God is "in here" with us, in the makeup of every cell, every motor neuron, every thought, every emotion. Everything is in God, and God is in everything. So in our quest for scientific and medical truth, we enter more fully into the Mystery we call God, regardless of which religion we espouse.

I've got to tell you, *TIME* is not on my side. But *HOPE* is. That is why I titled my previous book *LOTS OF HOPE . . . .* There never was a *NIGHT* or a *PROBLEM* that could defeat *SUNRISE* or *HOPE*.

I love how my friend William Sloane Coffin put it:

"All saving ideas are born small. God comes to earth as a child so that we can finally grow up—which means we can stop blaming God for being absent when we ourselves were not present, stop blaming God for the ills of the world as if we had been laboring to cure them, and stop making God responsible for all the thinking and doing that we should be undertaking on our own."

ALS research is often long and hard, frustrating and disappointing. But as Martin Luther King, Jr. said, "We must accept finite disappointment, but we must NEVER LOSE HOPE. . . . If you lose hope, somehow you lose the vitality that keeps life moving, you lose the courage to be—that quality that helps you go on in spite of it all. And so today, "I Still Have a Dream!"

I still have a dream. I think that what the Jewish prophet Jeremiah said 3,000 years ago needs to be said again today: "Surely I know the plans for you," says the Lord, "plans for your welfare and not for harm, to give you a future with hope."

"Dum Spiro, Spero" . . . "While I Breathe, I Hope." Every day there is some new discovery or insight. Having Hope doesn't make it better. Having Hope makes us want to make it better.

Two years before his assassination, Robert Kennedy spoke to thousands of students at the University of Cape Town in South Africa:

> *"It is from numberless diverse acts of courage and belief that human history is shaped," he said. "Each time a person stands up for an ideal, or acts to improve the lot of others, or strikes out against injustice, that person sends forth a tiny ripple of hope, and crossing each other from a million different centers of energy and daring, those ripples build a current which can sweep down the mightiest walls of oppression and resistances."*[83]

The person who has a *why* to live can put up with just about any *how*.

They say that they built the train tracks over the Alps between Venice and Vienna before there was a train that could make the trip. But they built it anyway . . . *because they knew the train would come!*

So, lots of *faith* to you, lots of *hope*, and especially, lots of *love!*

—GARY

NOTES

YOU DON'T SING ME LOVE SONGS ANYMORE . . .

1. The Church of Jesus Christ of Latter Day Saints, *Sunstone*, September, 1996.
2. Alan & Marilyn Bergman, "You Don't Bring Me Flowers," (Stonebridge Music & Threesome Music Company/ASCAP), duet sung by Barbra Streisand and Neil Diamond.
3. Charles B. Cousar, et al., *Texts for Preaching—Year C* (Louisville, KY: Westminster John Knox Press, 1994), pp. 127-129.
4. Joan Withers Priest, "Living Within a Covenant: The Sixth Commandment: 'You Shall Not Commit Adultery,'" sermon preached at the First Presbyterian Church of New Canaan, CT, August 3, 1997.

LOVE NEVER DIES

5. Rachel Naomi Remen, M.D., *My Grandfather's Blessings: Stories of Strength, Refuge, and Belonging* (New York, NY: The Berkley Publishing Group, 2000).
6. Harold S. Kushner, *Overcoming Life's Disappointments* (New York, NY: Alfred A. Knopf, 2006).
7. Jay Cormier, *Connections*, February 18, 2007, p. 3.

A LOVE STORY (FOR NATE AND THEO)

8. Sheldon Harnick, *Fiddler on the Roof*, 1964.
9. I Corinthians 13:13.
10. M. Scott Peck, *The Road Less Traveled* (New York, NY: Simon & Schuster, 1978), p. 81.
11. William Shakespeare, Sonnet 116.
12. Romans 8:35, 37-39.
13. Robert Browning, "Rabbi ben Ezra."
14. Fern G. Dunlap, "The Wedding Prayer."
15. Dr. Dean Ornish, cited by Rabbi Harold S. Kushner in *Living a Life That Matters: Resolving the Conflict between Conscience and Success* (New York, NY: Alfred A. Knopf, 2001), pp. 112, 113.
16. Delores Curran, *Traits of a Healthy Family* (Minneapolis, MN: Winston Press, 1984).
17. Ellen Goodman & Patricia O'Brien, *I Know Just What You Mean*, cited by Harold S. Kushner, *Living a Life That Matters*, op. cit., p. 117.
18. Mark 12:29-31.

19. Henri J. M. Nouwen, *Sabbatical Journey: The Diary of His Final Year* (New York, NY: Crossroad Publishing Company, 1998).

20. Martin Buber, cited by Harold S. Kushner, *Living a Life That Matters*, op cit., pp. 124, 125.

WHERE LOVE REIGNS

21. I John 4:16b

22. I Corinthians 13:13

23. David R. Hawkins, *Power vs. Force: The Hidden Determinants of Human Behavior*, cited by Gail Rogers, *The Bible Workbench*, (St. Louis, MO: The Educational Center), Vol. 14, Issue 4, p. 53.

24. C. G. Jung, *Two Essays on Analytical Psychology*, 2nd Edition (Princeton, NJ: Princeton University Press, Bolingen Foundation, 1966), p. 53.

25. Dorothy Bass, *Receiving the Day: Christian Practices for Opening the Gift of Time* [E-Book] (Jossey-Bass—Wiley Publishing Co., 2002).

DON'T YOU THINK IT'S TIME WE WENT UPSTREAM?

26. Tom Stella, *A Faith Worth Believing: Finding New Life Beyond the Rules of Religion* (San Francisco, CA: Harper Collins Publisher, 2004), p. 115.

27. Ibid., p. 122.

28. Ibid.

29. Reinhold Neibuhr, *The Irony of American History* (Chicago, IL: University of Chicago Press, 1952).

30. Clyde Haberman, NYC, "Integration, One Sunday at a Time," *The New York Times*, January 13, 2001, Metro Section, p. B1.

31. Robert Burns, "A Winter's Night."

32. William Sloane Coffin, *The Courage to Love* (San Francisco, CA: Harper & Row Publishers, 1984), p. 11.

PUTTING LOVE TO WORK

33. Andrea Rock, "You Can Remake Your Life," *Money Magazine*, December, 1997.

34. Richard W. Carlson, "Not Choosing, But Being Chosen," *The Christian Ministry*, January-February 1994, p. 11.

35. Michael Novak, *Business As a Calling* (New York, NY: The Free Press, 1996), p. 15.

36. Dennis Bakke, quoted by Suzy Wetlaufer, "Organizing for Empowerment: An Interview with AES's Roger Sant and Dennis Bakke," *Harvard Business Review*, January-February, 1999, pp. 120, 121.

37. Michael Novak, op. cit., p. 37.

LESSONS FROM THE TRAVELER'S WELCOME HOTEL

38. Trevanian, *Incident at Twenty-Mile* (New York, NY: St. Martin's Press, 1998), p. 127.

39. William Sloane Coffin, *The Heart Is a Little to the Left* (Dartmouth College, Hanover & London: University Press of New England, 1999), pp. 12-15.
40. Hosea 2:19-20.

DON'T GIVE UP ON LOVE

41. Douglas R. A. Hare, *Matthew, Interpretation Commentary* (Louisville, KY: John Knox Press, 1993), pp. 8-12.
42. John Shelby Spong, *A New Christianity for a New World: Why Traditional Faith Is Dying & How a New Faith Is Being Born* (San Francisco, CA: HarperSanFrancisco, 2001), pp. 139-141.
43. Carl Hulse, "First-Time Fatherhood at 57 Brings a New Perspective," National Report, *The New York Times*, October 22, 2001, p. A12.
44. "O Come, All Ye Faithful," "Adeste Fideles" written by John Francis Wade (1711-1786).

"GOD LOVES THE WHOLE WORLD . . . NO EXCEPTIONS"

45. James Turner, *Without God, Without Creed: The Origins of Unbelief in America*, (Baltimore, MD: The Johns Hopkins University Press, 1985), p. XI.
46. Albert B. Paine, *Mark Twain, A Biography: The Personal & Literary Life of Samuel Langhorne Clemens*, 1912.
47. William Sloane Coffin, Jr., "Our Role in the Incarnation," sermon preached at Riverside Church, New York City, NY, December 18, 1983
48. Michael Turpin, "God, Church and Construction Sites," *New Canaan News-Review*, "Perspective," Thursday, November 16, 2006, p. A21.
49. John Shelby Spong, op. cit., pp. 180-182.

DIAMONDS IN THE NIGHT

50. Charles Dickens, *A Christmas Carol* (New York, NY: Holiday House, 1923), pp. 82-83.

"YES, VIRGINIA, THERE IS A CHRIST CHILD"

51. Frederick Buechner, "Christmas Miracle: Beyond the Plastic, Still the Grace," from *Whistling in the Dark* (San Francisco, CA: Harper & Row, 1988).
52. Howard Thurman, Prologue to *The Mood of Christmas* (Richmond, IN: Friends United Press, 1985).

PAYING IT FORWARD AT CHRISTMAS

53. Roger Ebert, "Pay It Forward," *Chicago Sun-Times*, October 20, 2000.
54. Suggested by "God Comes From Within" by Kathy Coffey, *Eucharistic Minister*, Celebration Publications, December, 1987.
55. Colossians 1:27

56. Meister Eckhart, *Meditations with Meister Eckhart*, ed. Matthew Fox (Bear & Company Publishing, 1983).

57. Ann Weems, *Kneeling in Bethlehem* (Philadelphia, PA: The Westminster Press, 1980), p. 61.

58. Isaac Watts, "Joy to the World," *The Psalms of David*, 1719.

THE OUTRAGE OF LIGHT

59. Henry Wadsworth Longfellow, "Christmas Bells," 1863.

60. John 1:1-5

61. Matthew Joseph Thaddeus Stepanek, "Pinch of Peace," written in 1998, *Heart Songs* (New York, NY: Hyperion Books, 2002), p.24.

"IT'S A WONDERFUL LIFE"

62. Frank Capra, *The Name Above the Title* (New York, NY: The Macmillan Press, 1971), p. 375.

63. II Corinthians 8:9.

64. Jeanine Basinger, "From Frank Capra," *The It's A Wonderful Life Book* (New York, NY: Alfred A. Knopf, 1986), p. IX.

65. John 1:14.

THE AMAZING POWER OF YES

66. June M. Schulte, excerpted from Elizabeth Rankin Geitz, Marjorie A. Burke, and Ann Smith, eds., *Women's Uncommon Prayers: Our Lives Revealed, Nurtured, Celebrated* (Harrisburg, PA: Morehouse Publishing, 2000), pp. 286-87.

67. Meister Eckhart, *Die deutschen Werke*, ed. J. Quint (Stuttgart, Berlin,1936), *"Speech"* 4, DWI, pp. 69-70.

68. Colossians 1:26, 27.

69. John Shelby Spong, op. cit., pp. 139-140.

70. William Sloane Coffin, *A Passion for the Possible: A Message to U.S. Churches* (Louisville, Kentucky: Westminster/John Knox Press, 1993), p. 10.

THE TWELVE DAYS OF CHRISTMAS

71. William Sloane Coffin, "Epiphany," a meditation given on January 4, 1987, at Riverside Church, New York City.

72. Alfred Lord Tennyson (1809-1892), "In Memoriam A.H.H", Section CVI, 1850.

THE GREAT GIVE-AWAY: A CHRISTMAS STORY FOR ADULTS

73. Ray Buckley, *The Give-Away* (Nashville, TN: Abingdon Press, 1999).

74. John 3:16; I John 4:7-10.

ANGELS OF LIGHT

75. William Willimon, "Messengers of God.

76. Anthony Lewis, "Light in the Darkness," *The New York Times*, December 9, 1996, Op Ed Section, p. A17, reprinted November 11, 2009.

77. Isaiah 61:1, 4, 11b.

78. Ann Weems, "Wouldn't It Be Grand to Be an Angel?" *Kneeling in Bethlehem* (Philadelphia, PA: The Westminster Press, 1980), p. 40.

SANTA IS MY SON

79. Ruth Dalton, *Catholic Digest.*

80. Marcus J. Borg, *Reading the Bible Again for the First Time* (San Francisco, CA: Harper, 2001), pp. 34, 35.

81. John Shelby Spong, op. cit., p. 179.

82. John 3:16.

EPILOGUE

83. Robert F. Kennedy, "Day of Affirmation," address at the University of Capetown, South Africa, June 6, 1966. –*Congressional Record*, Volume 112, p. 12340.